The Funeral Service

David Saville

Hodder & Stoughton
LONDON SYDNEY AUCKLAND

500056028

British Library Cataloguing in Publication Data
A record for this book is available from the British Library.

ISBN 0 340 65183 0

Designed and typeset by Kenneth Burnley at Typograph,
Irby, Wirral, Cheshire.
Printed and bound in Great Britain by Cox & Wyman Ltd,
Reading, Berkshire

Hodder and Stoughton
A division of Hodder Headline PLC
338 Euston Road
London NW1 3BH

*This book is dedicated to the memory of Cyril and Frank,
my father and father-in-law.
Through their deaths in 1992
I experienced more than ever before in my life
the pain of bereavement.
In their funerals I appreciated more than ever before
the need to proclaim and hold on to
the wonderful Christian hope of eternal life.*

Contents

❧ Foreword
by the Bishop of Edmonton

IN A WORLD in which so much is uncertain, one thing is sure: death comes to us all. Medical advances and modern technologies have made great strides in extending human life. But the fact remains that every human being must eventually embrace death.

However, if death is inevitable, not everyone welcomes it. In fact death has become the last great taboo of our society. We don't like to talk about it, we don't know how to respond to it, we would rather change the subject.

I believe the Church has a unique opportunity and indeed responsibility to help society face death with confidence. The Church of England continues to provide funeral services for the large majority of people in this country. We can offer the services of parish priests who are skilled in pastoral care and in the conduct of funerals; the support of countless churchgoers whose faith enables them to comfort those engulfed by grief; and we can offer the hymns and prayers of a people united in their experience of a living Lord, Jesus Christ, who conquered death and rose from the grave.

I am delighted to commend this book by the Revd David Saville, my Adviser for Evangelism in the Edmonton Area. It is clear, warmly pastoral, and firmly rooted in the Gospel. I am sure very many will benefit from it.

✠ *Brian Edmonton*
November 1995

CHAPTER 1

❧ From here to eternity

An introduction

THIS BOOK is intended to be very much a popular 'consumer guide' to funeral services; it does not assume that its readers are regular worshippers or have a firm Christian faith or a detailed grasp of theology. My aim has been to avoid being too technical or complicated in language or ideas.

I realise that the book is likely to be particularly valuable for people in the middle of coping with deep feelings. Some will be facing the pain and grief of bereavement; others the anxiety about their own health, death, mortality (and therefore perhaps setting out their wishes for their own funeral); others the perplexity about funerals they have attended but which they did not really understand or perhaps found uninspiring or even discouraging.

These are the people I have mainly in mind in writing this book. Therefore it is not an academic theological work, although there will be reference to key ideas such as eternal life, heaven and resurrection; what Christians believe about them, and why. The funeral service speaks about the future of those who have died as well as the future of the bereaved as they adjust to a new situation in their lives. The service aims to help people make some sense of what has happened. If the Christian religion has nothing meaningful to say about death and eternity, it has nothing much to say at all.

The book is not a detailed liturgical study of the services produced by the different denominations, although it refers to several of them (and also to that prepared by the ecumenical Joint

11

Liturgical Group and included in the service book available at many crematoria). It is not written for Christian ministers as a guide to the history or meaning of the text or to how the service should be taken; there are several other books which meet this need.

This book does not go into detail about how to cope with bereavement or what to do when someone dies, although it touches on both those subjects. The funeral service can play a key part in coming to terms with the death of a loved person, and often the more one is involved in the service and in the planning of it the more helpful it can be in the bereavement process.

The main purposes of this book are:

1. To help people plan and prepare for a service for a close relative or friend

Often there is such a short time to do this following the death, but occasionally in cases of terminal illness plans can be made ahead and perhaps the dying person can be involved in making them. This can be a strengthening and positive experience. It is important to realise you have options to decide on, choices to make. There is a sense in which you can take control and take responsibility for the service. Of course often the bereaved find it hard to make any decisions at a time of shock and sorrow. However, to accept the 'package' suggested by the funeral director or clergy or simply to leave the details to them may produce a service which in retrospect was not really what you or the deceased would have chosen.

This book sets out some of the options. It is not an exhaustive resource book for funerals (a few such books are listed in Appendix A), but reference is made to a variety of Psalms, readings, hymns and prayers. Apart from the decision about burial or cremation (often the deceased will have stated their preference), there is the question of whether to have a service in church before going on to the crematorium or cemetery. (There is an increasing trend to have the committal at the crematorium/cemetery before a church service on the same day or at a later stage.) Most funeral directors would assume you are going 'straight to the crematorium', some may not mention the option, and a few would even discourage the idea of using the local church unless you or the deceased had strong links.

However, it is a real option, and if you are wanting a Christian service at all, as most people still do, it is certainly not hypocritical to choose a service in a church – and even some of the extra ceremonies, such as a vigil in church the previous evening (see Chapter 11). A church service has several advantages. First, it usually enables more members of the local community to attend which means you can feel encouraged by their presence. Second, it can be a more uplifting setting for a service which marks the journey of the deceased 'from here to eternity' and also hopefully lifts our attention to eternal things and to the God we turn to for strength and comfort. A third reason is to avoid a sense of rush which can be felt at a crematorium with the usual 'twenty minutes maximum' service, however well the service is taken. You can be very aware of the tight chapel timetable, with mourners leaving from the previous service and those arriving for the next. A funeral in church may not in fact be much longer than in a crematorium chapel, but it can feel special and more dignified.

It is true that relatives often request 'just a short simple service' either for physical reasons, for example some elderly mourners might find it very difficult to cope with the walking and travelling involved in going to church and then to the crematorium or cemetery, or for emotional reasons. Mourners may be very anxious about how they will survive the service. At the end of this chapter is a 'Postscript' about 'emotion in the funeral service'. However, looking back on the service later, what matters most is not the length of service or where it was held, but whether it gave opportunity to say to God what was in your heart, and to hear again about God's love for you at a time of pain and loss; and whether it did justice to, and celebrated, the life of the person you have lost.

Let me encourage you, if you have the whole service at the crematorium, to ask for a local minister to take the service, rather than leave it to someone on the rota there. It is so important to personalise the service; and a local minister, even if they have never met you before, can visit and find out about the deceased, and therefore tailor the whole service (not just the address) for this particular person.

2. To help people plan their own funeral service

An increasing number of people put down their wishes on paper. No doubt relatives and friends are enormously grateful to have clear guidelines rather than trying to remember what may or may not have been said or hinted at. 'Now, what were her favourite hymns?' 'I wonder if he did have a preference for burial or cremation?' If two of the keys to a helpful funeral service are making choices from the options available and personalising the service, then your instructions can be vital. Some may be reading this and planning their service because old age or serious illness make them realise death could be around the corner. I hope that, as you read about the various alternatives, and about the meaning of the funeral service and the Christian faith which undergirds it, you will find new strength and confidence to face the future.

For others, death may seem a more distant prospect, but you are taking the opportunity of making your wishes known about your funeral at the same time as drawing up your will or joining a pre-paid funeral scheme. (Appendix B sets out a check-list of things to decide on.) To plan your funeral is to be reminded of your mortality; a mixture of emotions may well be churning around in you – hope, anticipation, fear, anxiety.

Some of the anxiety may be about how, after your death, your relatives and friends will cope with life in general and with the funeral service in particular. Remember that if you have been loved you will be missed; there *will* be the inevitable grief and mourning and you cannot insulate others from that. At a recent service it was announced by a member of the family, 'He left instructions that we should not mourn his death.' An instruction like that is impossible to carry out! Mourning is a universal and natural reaction and cannot be so easily sidelined.

Similarly, if your instructions for your funeral are for a 'simple service' in order to protect your family and friends, you may be doing them a disservice. Grieving has to take its course and the funeral can be an important step in the process. There is the balance in a funeral service between remembering and reflecting the life of the deceased and meeting the needs of the mourners; in leaving instructions for your funeral, which the family will want to follow faithfully, it may be wise to leave some leeway for changes and suggestions which they might like to make.

3. To help people who have attended a Christian funeral service to explore the meaning and significance of it all and to explore the validity of the faith and hope expressed there

For an increasing number of people, religious language can sound like a foreign language, and religious ideas seem strange and out-dated. Even those brought up in the Christian faith or attending church from time to time may not have had the chance to think through the Christian view of death and resurrection which is found in the service – and which is not argued or explained there (except perhaps briefly in the address) but simply declared.

It is all the harder to take on board the meaning of the service if you are a very close relative or friend, and the service can be something of a blur. Little is remembered and, as many comment, 'It seemed unreal.'

Unfortunately, another factor making it difficult to take hold of the Christian message in the service may be the way in which the minister leads the service. Whatever the words which are spoken, the way in which the service is led can speak volumes. The Christian hope should be proclaimed with confidence and joy, the mourners addressed with a concern and understanding which mirrors something of God's care and comfort for them, the deceased referred to by name and with warmth and detail which come from careful enquiries, if not personal knowledge. But it is not always so. It is distressing to write this, and of course most funerals are very helpfully taken, but the impact of encountering an exception to the rule can be devastating and make it harder to believe that the Christian faith is worth a serious look.

It was to improve the church's ministry to the dying and the bereaved (in this and many other ways) that the Bishop of Edmonton's project 'Dying to Live' was undertaken in 1993–5. During the project I visited the home of a woman whom I had first met after a Sunday morning service in north London. After a gap of many years, Peggy had returned to church because of her distress at a funeral of a next-door neighbour. It was held at the crematorium and felt 'a cold service' because of the rather stark chapel, the fact that the neighbour was not known by the minister, and regrettably the way the service was taken. The experience could have driven her further from the Church and the faith. However, Peggy realised she wanted one day to have her funeral in a church where she belonged and was known, and where the service could be warm, personal and positive. So she began to worship again, made good friends, and felt better spiritually. She has now planned, and paid for, her funeral – 'a traditional rather than just a simple one'.

 ## POSTSCRIPT
Emotion in the funeral service

Many of us are frightened and embarrassed by our own strong emotions, and even more so by other people's. At a time of bereavement, when very strong emotions are present, whether or not we acknowledge them and express them, there may be the fear that they will get 'out of control', particularly at the funeral. 'I must be brave', 'I must try to be strong', 'I mustn't make a fool of myself' are the kind of comments the bereaved often make. Members of the family may be worried whether one or two of them will be able to cope with the service. Therefore the request for 'Something as short and simple as possible' is understandable.

However, it is exceedingly rare for a service to be interrupted or seriously disturbed by displays of emotion. Furthermore, no one really wants a clinical, impersonal or rushed service which disregards the dignity of the occasion, the sorrow of the mourners or the value of the person who has died. Yes, there may need to be some self-control during the service, so long as this does not rule out any tears, or become a reluctance to express publicly the deep emotions of grief and loss (and perhaps anger and guilt and fear) in the months which follow.

In my experience, there are many people who wish they had felt more at the service. They were still dazed and numb in what is usually a very early stage of bereavement (within a week or ten days). They can even regret that it felt unreal; something shattering has happened, but because of the shock, 'It hasn't really hit me yet.' This is entirely natural. It will be important for these people, as for those who to some extent have to restrain their feelings at a funeral, to have opportunities in later months and even years for sharing and expressing such feelings beyond their own private, and perhaps very lonely, world.

There is of course a cultural element in all this. For example, at an Afro-Caribbean funeral (and in the days beforehand), there is a more natural and expected place for wailing and crying as an expression of their grief. This must be helpful and therapeutic. Different races and faiths have their own customs. The main danger is denial; denial of what has happened or of our own feelings and reactions.

CHAPTER 2

❧ Here are the headlines

Sentences and prayers

THE FIRST WORDS of the service are likely to be these words of Jesus Christ from John's gospel: 'I am the resurrection and the life. He who believes in me will live, even though he dies, and whoever lives and believes in me will never die.' This verse is usually followed by other sentences of Scripture which immediately focus our attention on the basis of the Christian hope and the nature of the God to whom we pray in the service.

It is a bold, even dramatic, opening to the funeral. It immediately sets the scene, putting the service in the context of what Christians believe; it sounds a note of assurance about God's love and mercy, and about eternal life. If you are not used to a funeral service, it may even come as quite a surprise. It is as if the minister is declaring before anything else is said or done, 'Here are the headlines: death is not the end; there is resurrection and life available through Jesus Christ.'

In practice it may sometimes be difficult, particularly for the chief mourners, to take in what is being said. Usually the sentences are read by the minister leading in the coffin and the mourners from the door of the church or crematorium chapel. It is not an easy time to concentrate on the words. There is all the uncertainty and apprehension about the service, the natural distress at seeing the coffin, and the questions in one's mind such as 'Where exactly are we going to sit?' and 'Who has come along to the service?'

One helpful alternative might be for all the congregation, including the immediate family, to be seated in church first, with a chance to pray quietly and listen to the organ, before the minister leads in the coffin and uses the Scripture sentences. A second alternative (if the service is in church) is for the coffin to be there before the service begins, perhaps brought in the night before with a short service (see Chapter 11). A third alternative is for the minister to wait until everyone is in their place before starting the sentences. If you are involved in planning a service, these are options to consider; they might enable people to give better attention to 'the headlines' and to be encouraged by them.

Now we will take a look at some of the 'sentences of Scripture' from the Bible which are most commonly used. In some cases they will be heard again later in the service as part of a Psalm (see Chapter 3) or one of the readings (see Chapter 4).

As the verses are read one after another, it is impossible in the service to do more than take hold of the immediate encouragement and comfort from some of these 'sentences of Scripture'. However, reflecting on them and considering their context, as we can here, reinforces their significance for those coping with death and bereavement.

> Jesus said 'I am the resurrection and the life. He who believes in me will live, even though he dies; and whoever lives and believes in me will never die.'
>
> (John 11:25–6)

It was four days after the funeral of Lazarus, a close friend of Jesus and brother of Martha and Mary. They lived at Bethany near Jerusalem. Jesus was not present at the funeral; when he heard news of Lazarus' illness it was already too late for him to get there in time. Both sisters felt that if Jesus had been there earlier he could have healed Lazarus and prevented his death. Their comments are echoed by the thoughts and questions of so many who mourn: 'If only . . .', 'Why?', 'Perhaps it could have been prevented.' Their deep grief is shared by Jesus; later in the chapter we read 'Jesus wept' (v. 35).

In this situation both Jesus and Martha spoke about resurrection. Martha believed in a resurrection of the dead 'at the last day'. Jesus does not deny that, but declares (in the verses used in the funeral service) that he is the source of resurrection and life, and therefore to believe in him makes all the difference now to our life and to our death. ('Believe' means more than acknowledging his existence; it is a trusting in him, an entrusting of ourselves to him.) Those who believe will not be immune to physical death but can be sure they 'will live'. In fact Jesus claims that the life which comes through a relationship with him is eternal; so, believers 'will never die' in the sense of ever losing contact with God, even though their bodies fail and die.

As a sign or parable of what he meant, Jesus brought Lazarus back to life. It was not like the resurrection of Jesus himself; Lazarus returned to continue his life here and in due course he no doubt died once again. However, Jesus showed his power over death and pointed forward to a resurrection beyond death.

These are not easy verses to understand. Their meaning is rich and deep. But it is not hard to see why they are the traditional start to the service. Death and grief are not denied, but here is hope of eternal life.

> The eternal God is our refuge, and underneath are the ever-lasting arms.
>
> (Deuteronomy 33:27)

Now we are back in the Old Testament. Shortly before his death, Moses is portrayed as blessing the different tribes of Israel in turn. Then there is a final song of praise describing God in terms which should give confidence to the whole of Israel about their future in the 'promised land'! The song draws upon their earlier experience of 'the exodus', when God rescued them from slavery in Egypt.

These words continue to be a source of strength to many. In all the changes of life and in the grief of death and bereavement, God remains 'eternal'. He is a refuge, a place of shelter and safety in the storm; and because he is eternal so is his support of us – 'underneath are the everlasting arms'. The Bible often describes

God in very human terms so that we can get the message. His 'arms' are always there to hold us up; like a parent with a young child struggling to walk, or a friend with someone learning to swim. Perhaps at a funeral we feel the need of his 'arms' to be like those of someone getting a firm hold on a drowning person in a raging sea. The famous 'Footprints' reading (see page 73) is relevant here.

> The steadfast love of the Lord never ceases, his compassion never fails: every morning they are renewed.
>
> (Lamentations 3:22, 23)

Here is another Old Testament passage which speaks of God's constant reliability. His love and compassion never cease or fail. The remarkable thing about these verses is that they were written following a great national tragedy – the fall of the city of Jerusalem in 587 BC and the deportation of many Jews to the foreign territory of Babylon. It was an ancient example of what today would be called ethnic cleansing. The writer expresses deep anguish and distress, but also despite everything this amazing hope in God.

These may seem hard verses to hold on to in any bereavement and particularly when someone has died young or in tragic circumstances. Wonderfully, at such a time, many do experience God's compassion, often through the care of family and friends around them, but also in the gift of peace or reassurance deep inside them.

For the Christian, the words take on added significance, because God's love and compassion are displayed supremely in the life and death of Jesus, and also because the Easter message of resurrection points to the fact that his love and compassion towards us will never cease for all eternity.

We continue with three verses from the Psalms. These are not printed in the Church of England service but appear in other services, including the one produced by the Joint Liturgical Group (representing different churches) and are printed in the book commonly used at a crematorium.

> Cast your burdens on the Lord, and he will sustain you.
>
> > (Psalm 55:22)

Psalm 55 is a Psalm of David in which he cries out to God, 'My thoughts trouble me and I am distraught' (v. 2) and 'My heart is in anguish within me; the terrors of death assail me' (v. 4). We can identify with his feelings even if his situation was very different – facing personal enemies and the betrayal of a friend.

Then, near the end of the Psalm, David encourages others to do what he has done in such turmoil. The promise is not that God will take over the burden, but that 'he will sustain you' in carrying it. There's an echo here of the phrase in the Deuteronomy verse about the arms of God underneath us. The pain, sorrow and sense of loss will not suddenly go away, but we can be strengthened through such a time. In the New Testament, Peter was probably quoting part of the verse when he wrote 'Cast all your anxieties on him because he cares for you' (1 Peter 5:7).

> God is our refuge and strength, a very present help in trouble.
>
> > (Psalm 46:1)

At a time of 'trouble' or crisis, when everything around us seems to be collapsing, our security can still be in God; that's the theme of this Psalm. The next verse reads,

> therefore we will not fear,
>   though the earth give way
> and the mountains fall into
>   the heart of the sea.

This is a powerful picture of a situation in which everything seems to be disintegrating and those things we relied on are removed. Even at such a time God can be our shelter and strength. The description of him as 'a very present help' points to his help being sufficient for any predicament. Christians link this idea with the teaching of Jesus to call God 'our Father'. Earthly fathers are often unreliable, not always ready to be bothered or able to help, but our heavenly Father is 'an ever-present help'.

> In God's favour is life; weeping may endure for a night, but joy comes in the morning.
>
> (Psalm 30:5)

A verse from a Psalm of gratitude and praise to God because 'you lifted me out of the depths' (v. 1). David looked back to what was a time of great anxiety but it did not last for ever. So the Psalmist drew the contrast between a temporary period of 'weeping' and the 'rejoicing' which eventually returned. Of course it is not always helpful to be told that 'it won't last for ever' when you are in the thick of it, and there seems no light at the end of the tunnel. It is much easier, when everything feels so much better, to look back on a painful time, as David did. However, the New Testament encourages us to see the contrast here in terms of the momentary and the eternal; we can put our present troubles alongside the hope of life after death, of resurrection, of life which can be lived to the full. St Paul, in his letter to the Romans, put it like this: 'I consider that our present sufferings are not worth comparing with the glory that will be revealed in us' (Romans 8:18).

> Blessed are those who mourn, for they shall be comforted.
>
> (Matthew 5:4)

After a number of Old Testament verses, we are back with the words of Jesus Christ. Here is one of the 'beatitudes', part of his teaching to his followers in what is often called 'the Sermon on the Mount'. Of all the sentences of Scripture which can be used at this part of the service, this is the one most easily misunderstood unless we remember the context. It is not simply repeating the truth from Psalm 30:5 that weeping will turn into joy, or affirming that in the world to come there will be compensation for the difficulties, inequalities and 'unfairness' of life here. It is indeed true, as the book of Revelation states, that 'there will be no more death, or mourning or crying or pain' (21:4), and this is a wonderful part of the Christian hope. It is also true that the bereaved can know the comfort which comes from God, in this life, as well as the next. The funeral service itself may be one means by which this comfort comes.

However, this verse in Matthew's gospel is one of a series of statements in which Jesus spoke to his disciples about what it means to follow him. They are 'blessed' or 'fortunate' or 'happy' because although their lives will involve mourning, there is the certainty of God's comfort, not as a reward or compensation but simply as part of what God delights to give to his people. Such mourning can take various forms; it will include bereavement but also distress over one's own life and over the state of the world. Jesus Christ gives people a greater sensitivity to sorrow and pain around them, as well as the hope of consolation and comfort. How valuable it is when those who attend a funeral to support the immediate mourners are people of such sensitivity and compassion.

> God so loved the world that he gave his only Son, that whoever believes in him should not perish but have eternal life.
>
> (John 3:16)

For many people, this is the most famous and best-loved verse in the Bible. It may be important, if you are planning a service, to ask the minister to ensure that this is included, and not to stop the sentences early just because the procession has finished! The verse has been called the heart of the Gospel, the Christian 'Good News'. Some may remember the posters at the football world cup matches simply proclaiming 'John 3:16'; a rather cryptic message, but perhaps a prompt to some to take hold again of a truth which they had heard about or even once believed in.

Here are two basic themes in John's gospel and in the whole Christian faith: the love of God for his whole world, and the gift of eternal life. God's love is practical and sacrificial; it results in the coming of his Son as a human being, and that human life of Jesus of Nazareth is the most powerful demonstration of the love of God, particularly in facing suffering and crucifixion. God intervened in this way in order that people might receive 'eternal life'. This means both life in the world to come but refers also to a quality of life which can be received from God and enjoyed with God now.

From the start of the Christian Church, these truths, centring on the death and resurrection of Jesus, have transformed people's attitude to death. This is why they are so relevant to a funeral service. There is still grief and sorrow but, as St Paul put it, we do 'not grieve as others do who have no hope' (1 Thessalonians 4:13). Hope is one of the great Christian words, indicating something which is sure and reliable rather than merely wishful thinking or 'hoping against hope'. The meaning and the basis for the Christian hope will be explored further, particularly in the chapters on readings and hymns (pages 47 & 80ff).

The great news is that eternal life is given to those who simply believe in the Son of God; if such a gift were only for those whose lives deserved it, no one would have a chance! Of course there is also that dark side to John 3:16, expressed in the word 'perish'. This is the other side of the coin: the assumption that not all will avoid the possibility of perishing by putting their faith in Jesus Christ and what he has done for them. The good news is that God enables anyone to experience eternal life; the bad news is that some may choose not to. It is a doctrine which many find difficult to believe, preferring instead a 'universalism', i.e. all people go to heaven. But most Christians still hold to the idea of hell, even though they wish they did not have to (see the Postscript at the end of this chapter).

Despite this aspect to the meaning of the verse, the overall thrust is of enormous hope and encouragement. This is true of all these 'sentences of Scripture' which begin the service. They are like banner headlines boldly proclaiming what God is like for those who turn to him at such a difficult time. Together with the opening prayer or prayers which usually follow, they set the scene, even if not everyone present is able emotionally or spiritually at that moment to 'take on board' all that is being said.

Opening prayers

The modern Anglican service has a prayer which is normally said together by the congregation and which acknowledges that God has 'given us a true faith and a sure hope' and asks for the strengthening of this faith and hope 'in us all our days'. Not everyone may feel able to say this, but the service is written to express the Christian faith and the assumption is that those who ask for a Christian funeral expect it to state unambiguously what Christians generally believe.

It would be almost impossible to draw up a service so full of 'perhaps' and 'maybe' that it made some allowance for everyone's doubts and the variety of outlook! For those arranging a funeral, there are other options than the Christian service. Some choose a service within a different religious tradition while, increasingly, others opt for a secular non-religious service if they or the deceased have rejected a faith in God – though such services are still a very small proportion of those taken in this country.

However, this still leaves us with the awkwardness at a Christian service when some are faced with the words which they cannot honestly say or sing. The answer is not to water down the Christian affirmations but for the way in which the service is led to be sensitive to where people stand; for example some ministers in addition to, or instead of, the address give an explanatory running commentary to the service which tries to address people's misunderstandings or doubts (see page 77).

The words in the opening prayer about 'a true faith and a sure hope' refer to faith and hope not as personal characteristics, but as aspects of the Christian Gospel. The emphasis is on their content and their basis in what God has done for the world, and promised to the world in Jesus Christ. (In the new draft Methodist service, an opening prayer states 'In the presence of death, Christ offers us sure ground for hope, confidence and joy.') Following on from this, the petition 'strengthen this faith and hope in us' is more about the subjective and personal way in which we respond – '*My* faith', '*My* hope'. Everyone, even if they have been a Christian for a long time, needs this strengthening of faith and hope. They may have taken quite a knock because of the bereavement and the circumstances leading up to it, but the prayer is a reminder that a key element in coping with loss and grief is a strengthening of what we believe about God and the future. Therefore one of the main purposes of the service, from the sentences and prayers onwards, is to declare the content of this faith and hope, so that a fresh response can be made to it, even though it's such a traumatic time – or rather, *because* it is such a time.

 ## POSTSCRIPT
Heaven – and hell?

There are not two Christian funeral services: one for those we think are destined for heaven and another for those who will miss out! The service makes the assumption that those we commend to God's mercy will indeed be safe with him, and experience resurrection and eternal life.

Why this assumption? First, our belief in God's love for the whole world and not just for a few people. 'God so loved the world that he gave his one and only Son' (John 3:16). 'God our Saviour, who wants all men to be saved and to come to a knowledge of the truth' (1 Timothy 2:3–4). Second, the fact that we cannot know for certain where anyone stands in their relation to God at the end of life, even if we are their closest relative. Only God can fully know. It may seem that someone has rejected God, and wants nothing to do with him, but we do not know their heart, nor the factors in their life which may have made it so difficult to appreciate the existence or the mercy of God – factors which God however entirely understands. Therefore we entrust people to a God who judges with perfect knowledge and love and justice.

Some Christians would argue that we do not need to make an assumption about people's destiny; we can be sure everyone will go to heaven. Many others, while wishing that that were indeed the case, feel they must take seriously the warnings throughout the New Testament, and particularly in the words of Jesus himself, about the possibility of hell, of missing out on the life God offers to all.

It is hard to envisage or describe what hell is. We are not helped by the lurid medieval paintings and murals of judgment and hell. We must also realise that the New Testament metaphors and symbols, for example the Gehenna rubbish tip outside Jerusalem, are only pointers to the reality. We have to talk about hell in negative terms: separation from God, and from the full and fulfilling life we shall enjoy in heaven.

So, who might miss out? Let me start by answering the opposite question: Who goes to heaven? A common misunderstanding is to think that people deserve to get into heaven if they have lived quite good lives, never done much harm to others, and generally tried to do their best; and therefore hell is for the really evil people. The problem with this view is that it ignores the glory and perfect holiness of God, and also the fact that no one has kept the standards he has set down: to love God with all your heart, mind and strength, and to love your neighbour as yourself. It is therefore obvious now, and certainly will be so at 'the last judgment', that no one deserves to get into heaven.

This is why Christians believe that God came in Jesus Christ to save us, to rescue us from that predicament. He did not ignore or condone all that has happened in the world. He faced it head on, and took responsibility for putting it right – at the Cross. Instead of hope for no one, there is hope for everyone. It is on the basis not of what we deserve, but of God's love and mercy, which we need to trust in and accept for ourselves.

So, who might miss out? Not necessarily the worst people, who have performed such evil acts. They can be accepted by God in the same way as anyone else, if they genuinely turn to him and ask for mercy and forgiveness. The people who might miss out are those who reject the offer of mercy and life. In Luke chapter 18, Jesus told a parable about a religious and upright man who made the mistake of assuming he was righteous and good enough for God, and another man who knew his life was a mess and whose only prayer was 'God be merciful to me, a sinner.' The punchline was that the second man was accepted by God rather than the first.

You can understand why Christians regard sharing the Good News of 'salvation' as such a high priority. Of course not everyone has the chance to hear it. This is not their fault, and God will deal lovingly and justly with them, in the light of how they have responded to their consciences and to what they do know about God, and their awareness of needing his mercy and pardon. Others who never 'hear' the Gospel, but are of course safe with God, are those who die at a young age or have severe learning difficulties.

In the end, it comes down to people's own choices. The gift of free will is a precious gift from God to the people he has created; we are not machines, pre-programmed by God. He leaves us to decide, to choose. If some miss out on eternal life with God, it will be their choice, not his.

It is a deeply serious subject. But we conclude this note optimistically, because God has shown unmistakably that he loves us all to the limit, and that he wants us all to know him and live with him for ever.

CHAPTER 3

❧ Songs from the heart
Psalms

AT THIS POINT in the service, after the opening sentence
and prayer a Psalm is often said or sung. The Church of England
funeral service suggests a number of Psalms which could be used;
other forms of service, while not giving quite the same emphasis
to the Psalms, include some as possible passages of Scripture for
the 'reading' or 'lesson'.

In practice, the Psalm is usually read – by the minister
alone, or together with the congregation, or by them saying alter-
nate verses. It is much harder to sing the Psalms, although they
were originally written to be sung. If the funeral is in church, there
is occasionally a choir to chant the Psalm, giving the congregation
the chance to listen and reflect on the words. (For this, as for many
parts of the service, it helps enormously to have the words available in a service book or in a specially produced service sheet.)
Another option is for the congregation to sing a simple response
after each verse or two.

By far the most common way of singing a Psalm is to use a
hymn version (sometimes called a 'metrical version') and some of
the best known are mentioned in this chapter. They vary a great
deal in how far they retain the words, meaning and flow of the
original Psalm, but they are a way of making the Psalms more
accessible to many worshippers.

Why do we use an ancient Psalm in a modern funeral?
There are two paradoxical answers. One is their history, the fact
that they have been used by Jews and Christians for many centuries. They are sometimes referred to as 'the Psalms of David',

and some indeed are probably by King David and are therefore now three thousand years old. Others of the 150 Psalms were written over a long period of Old Testament history, particularly for the festivals and other worship in the Temple at Jerusalem.

The Psalms, well known and in regular use by Jesus and his earliest followers, are often quoted in the New Testament. They form the oldest hymn book (and song book) of the Christian Church, and had their place in Christian worship, including funeral services, from the earliest days.

The other reason for our use of the Psalms is how up-to-date they are! Even when we do not understand all the historical allusions, we recognise a universal language here; the different moods and feelings of the human heart and soul are expressed in ways which we can make our own. Many people feel they need to be polite and restrained in their prayer to God, even in private. But here are words which enable us, and encourage us, to articulate feelings which are around at a funeral: sorrow, depression, anger, betrayal, guilt, as well as simple trust, hope and praise. The Psalms are a wonderful resource for a funeral, as they are for church worship and private prayer more generally.

In this chapter we shall look at five of the most commonly used Psalms and four hymn-versions of them. Then we'll refer very briefly to three other Psalms which are listed in the service as possible alternatives.

Psalm 23

[1]The Lord is my shepherd, I shall not be in want:
[2] He makes me lie down in green pastures,
he leads me beside quiet waters,
[3] he restores my soul.
He guides me in paths of righteousness
    for his name's sake.
[4]Even though I walk
    through the valley of the shadow of death,
I will fear no evil,

　for you are with me;
your rod and your staff,
　they comfort me.

5You prepare a table before me
　in the presence of my enemies.
You anoint my head with oil;
　my cup overflows.
6Surely goodness and love will follow me
　all the days of my life,
and I will dwell in the house of the Lord
　for ever.

This must be the best loved of all the Psalms, and it is certainly a favourite at funerals either in one of the hymn versions or using the Bible passage itself. It is also a common choice for marriage services and I have known several instances where it was chosen for the funeral of a husband or wife because it brought back memories of their wedding.

The metaphor of the shepherd and sheep in the first four verses is increasingly removed from the experience of so many of us in a mainly urban society. Certainly the Eastern shepherd who lives with his sheep, leads, guides, protects them, even today in Israel, is someone we glimpse only in a documentary or, for a few, on a Holy Land tour. Despite this, the reflections of the Psalmist are true for many of us in a time of bereavement:

- the Psalm is very personal; the relationship of the Lord God with 'me', as 'my shepherd' is a firm reassurance that, when life seems to have lost its bearings, I still matter. God knows my situation, my grief, my needs.
- the promise of peace, stillness and refreshment (or restoration) for our souls answers a deep longing.
- at this moment we ourselves are walking 'through the valley of the shadow of death'. It is a place of deep shadow, a frightening journey. And yet . . . the Lord is with us to

strengthen, to comfort. I find it helpful to realise that although the shadow is produced by a hill or mountain which seems to dominate the scene, there is only shadow if there is light beyond. Psalm 27 reminds us 'the Lord is my light and my salvation'. Jesus said 'I am the light of the world' (John 8:12).

• the Lord is also the supreme host and friend (vv. 5–6). We shall more than survive the ordeal. There is so much still to enjoy; although we cannot be sure if the Psalmist had an eternal hope rather than a confidence in God's presence for the rest of his life, the end of the Psalm is developed by Jesus' words that 'in my father's house are many rooms (mansions)' (John 14:2).

Hymn: 'The Lord's my Shepherd'

The Lord's my Shepherd, I'll not want:
He makes me down to lie
In pastures green; He leadeth me
The quiet waters by.

My soul he doth restore again;
And me to walk doth make
Within the paths of righteousness,
E'en for His own name's sake.

Yea, though I walk in death's dark vale,
Yet will I fear none ill:
For Thou art with me; and Thy rod
And staff me comfort still.

My table Thou hast furnishèd
In presence of my foes;
My head Thou dost with oil anoint,
And my cup overflows.

Goodness and mercy all my life
Shall surely follow me;
And in God's house for evermore
My dwelling-place shall be.

This version of Psalm 23 was written in the sixteenth century and very accurately reproduces the ideas and words of the original. It is usually sung to the tune 'Crimond': indeed the hymn is often referred to by that name. It is certainly the most popular musical item at funerals. Organists at crematoria sometimes complain of having to play it at most of the funerals when they are on duty, but for many mourners its very familiarity enables them to express hopes and fears in the singing of it.

So, its popularity seems to grow. All that we have said about the relevance of the Psalm itself to people's moods and feelings at a funeral apply to this metrical version which gives so many mourners something immediately familiar in the middle of what can be a strange as well as stressful occasion.

Hymn: 'The King of love'

The King of love my Shepherd is,
Whose goodness faileth never;
I nothing lack if I am His
And He is mine for ever.

Where streams of living water flow
My ransomed soul He leadeth,
And where the verdant pastures grow
With food celestial feedeth.

Perverse and foolish oft I strayed
But yet in love He sought me,
And on His shoulder gently laid,
And home rejoicing brought me.

In death's dark vale I fear no ill
With Thee, dear Lord, beside me;
Thy rod and staff my comfort still,
Thy cross before to guide me.

Thou spread'st a table in my sight;
Thy unction grace bestoweth:
And O what transport of delight
From Thy pure chalice floweth!

And so through all the length of days
Thy goodness faileth never;
Good Shepherd, may I sing Thy praise
Within Thy house for ever.

This is another popular hymn based on Psalm 23. Sir Henry Baker, its author, was vicar of a small parish in Herefordshire in the mid-nineteenth century. This was a post which allowed him time to write many hymns and to take responsibility for the production of the best-known hymn book in the world, *Hymns Ancient and Modern.*

Unlike 'The Lord's my Shepherd', this hymn is not a straight paraphrase or metrical version of the Psalm which keeps as close as possible to the biblical text. It is obviously based on the Psalm but gives it a definitely Christian interpretation at several points, with echoes of the words of Jesus in the gospels.

The first verse emphasises the close relationship of the shepherd and sheep. In John's gospel, chapter 10, Jesus spoke of himself as the good shepherd who knows his sheep by name and keeps them safe 'for ever' – 'I give them eternal life . . . and no-one can snatch them out out of my hand' (v. 28).

In the second verse of the hymn, 'the quiet waters' become 'streams of living water', Jesus' own description of the life of his Spirit in his people, which is the guarantee and foretaste of eternal life (John 7:38).

The Psalmist's words 'He restores my soul' in the wonderful third verse are explained by a reference to Jesus' parable of the lost sheep which the shepherd hunts high and low for, until he finds it (Luke 15:3–7). The sheep may be the only one out of a hundred which wanders off, but the shepherd still searches for it; this is the value of each individual to the Lord, who as the good shepherd is even prepared to 'lay down his life for the sheep' (John 10:11). Hence, in the fourth verse, the reference to the cross of Christ. This part of the Psalm is so appropriate for a funeral. Sir Henry Baker keeps close to the original but adds this distinctively Christian emphasis: in the shadow of death it is the death of Christ for us which is the source of great light and hope.

Then the fifth verse becomes a reference to the Holy Communion, the Lord's table spread before us, where Christians draw strength from the One whose body was broken and blood poured out in costly love.

It is recorded that when Sir Henry Baker was himself dying, he repeated to himself the words 'Perverse and foolish oft I strayed . . .' The words of the hymn have brought strength and comfort to many others also at times of death or bereavement.

Psalm 90

1Lord, you have been our dwelling-place
   throughout all generations.
2Before the mountains were born
   or you brought forth the earth and the world,
   from everlasting to everlasting you are God.
3You turn men back to dust,
   saying, 'Return to dust, O sons of men.'
4For a thousand years in your sight
   are like a day that has just gone by,
   or like a watch in the night.
5You sweep men away in the sleep of death;
   they are like the new grass of the morning –
6though in the morning it springs up new,
   by evening it is dry and withered.

^{10}The length of our days is seventy years –
    or eighty, if we have the strength;
yet their span is but trouble and sorrow,
    for they quickly pass, and we fly away.

^{12}Teach us to number our days aright,
    that we may gain a heart of wisdom.

^{14}Satisfy us in the morning with your unfailing love,
    that we may sing for joy and be glad all our days.

^{16}May your deeds be shown to your servants,
    your splendour to their children.
^{17}May the favour of the Lord our God rest upon us;
    establish the work of our hands for us –
    yes, establish the work of our hands.

I have little doubt that this Psalm is rarely used at funerals in its original version, but of course the metrical version by Isaac Watts ('O God our help in ages past') is one of the most famous hymns in the English language, used both at funerals and times of national mourning and remembrance. Watts' paraphrase is based primarily on verses 1 to 6, but also reflects the hope expressed in 14, 16 to 17.

In the traditional *Book of Common Prayer*, Psalm 90 was one of only two Psalms appointed to be read at 'The Burial of the Dead' service. Today, although retained in some modern services, it is one of several alternatives and rarely used. Why is this? Presumably because it strikes a sober note: human life is brief, transitory, uncertain. Even at a funeral we can prefer to avoid the harsh facts of death and of our own mortality. But Psalm 90 does not allow us to avoid them.

Indeed, real wisdom comes in facing reality rather than avoiding it: 'Teach us to number our days' (v. 12). There is a prayer in the modern Church of England service which takes up this theme: 'Grant us Lord the wisdom and the grace to use aright the time that is left to us here on earth' (see Chapter 7, page 94).

Our brief life on earth is set alongside the eternal nature of God (v. 2). For him a thousand years are like a day (v. 4), whereas our life can seem like the grass which can wither and die so quickly (vv. 5–6). The contrast with the everlasting God not only sharpens the harsh realities of life and death; it is also the source of strength and hope. For generation after generation, he has been a refuge, shelter and dwelling place (v. 1). We seem to pass through this life as homeless and rootless people, but our 'dwelling place' can be in him.

Although the Lord is eternal, the Psalm does not deal with the hope of eternal life for the individual. Such a hope develops through the Old Testament and comes to full expression for Christians through the death and resurrection of Jesus. Isaac Watts includes this hope in his version of the Psalm.

Hymn: 'O God, our help in ages past'

O God, our help in ages past,
Our hope for years to come,
Our shelter from the stormy blast;
And our eternal home;

Under the shadow of Thy throne
Thy saints have dwelt secure;
Sufficient is Thine arm alone,
And our defence is sure.

Before the hills in order stood,
Or earth received her frame,
From everlasting Thou art God,
To endless years the same.

A thousand ages in Thy sight
Are like an evening gone,
Short as the watch that ends the night
Before the rising sun.

Time, like an ever-rolling stream,
Bears all its sons away;
They fly forgotten, as a dream
Dies at the opening day.

O God, our help in ages past,
Our hope for years to come,
Be Thou our guard while troubles last,
And our eternal home.

In his paraphrase, Watts does not spare us the harsh realities so powerfully alluded to in the Psalm itself. The fifth verse is almost overwhelming in its imagery and starkness – 'They fly forgotten . . .'

And yet . . . the hymn is so popular! I think there are three reasons for this, apart from the sheer quality of the writing itself. First, the tune 'St Anne', which seems to fit and express the words so well. Second, its association with great national occasions such as the Cenotaph service on Remembrance Sunday. It has become a kind of national anthem for bereavement and loss! Finally, Watts inserts the phrase 'our eternal home' in the first and last verses to express the hope of heaven and resurrection which is at the centre of the Christian faith. The Lord is not only a home, a dwelling place for succeeding generations during their brief pilgrimage of life on earth; we will find our home with him for eternity. As Jesus said, 'In my Father's house are many rooms' (John 14:2).

The 'stormy blast' of verse 1 may express something of what we feel as we sing this at a funeral, but the hymn gives us hope of God's help through it, and much more beyond.

Psalm 121

1I lift up my eyes to the hills –
    where does my help come from?
2My help comes from the Lord,
    the Maker of heaven and earth.
3He will not let your foot slip –

he who watches over you will not slumber;
4indeed, he who watches over Israel
will neither slumber nor sleep.
5The Lord watches over you –
the Lord is your shade at your right hand;
6the sun will not harm you by day,
nor the moon by night.
7The Lord will keep you from all harm –
he will watch over your life;
8the Lord will watch over your coming and going
both now and for evermore.

Here is a Psalm of firm confidence in the Lord to protect, defend, watch over us and all his people. The dark side of life is not ignored; on the contrary several verses refer, often in poetic language, to the risks and dangers we face. However, the overall message is that God can be trusted. Not surprisingly, at funerals and in other crises of life many people find it a magnificent way of expressing faith in a caring God – or a means of having such faith revived in them.

It is one of a block of Psalms (120–34) called the 'Songs of Ascents', i.e. for pilgrims going up to Jerusalem to worship at the Temple. This explains the reference to 'hills' in verse 1 – the hills around the city of Jerusalem and the hill on which it was built. But the thrust of this verse is not clear. Was it the danger lurking in the hills, for example robbers, which leads the pilgrims to put their trust in God again as their protector? Or was it, as many would echo today, the sight of the beauty of God's creation which drew them to the Creator who exercises his power in making 'heaven and earth' and also in the personal and wise care of his people?

It is very reassuring that at a time of shock, numbness and even despair the Lord is constantly awake (v. 4). In bereavement, the days can be long, and the nights even longer, but the Lord is present throughout both (v. 6). Verse 7 does not promise a trouble-free life, but protection and armour in the troubles.

The phrase in verse 8, 'going out and coming in' yields a

variety of meanings which can be appropriate at such a time, for example the beginning and end of life, special journeys and undertakings, and the simple routine of going out from one's home and returning to it. For those who have lost a partner, it can be the returning to the empty house which feels so painful, whether after a trip to the shops or a few days with relatives or friends. The 'coming in' can be dreaded and even avoided; here is a verse to hold on to at such a time.

Psalm 130

¹Out of the depths I cry to you, O Lord;
2   O Lord, hear my voice.
Let your ears be attentive
    to my cry for mercy.
³If you, O Lord, kept a record of sins,
    O Lord, who could stand?
⁴But with you there is forgiveness;
    therefore you are feared.
⁵I wait for the Lord, my soul waits,
    and in his word I put my hope.
⁶My soul waits for the Lord
    more than watchmen wait for the morning,
    more than watchmen wait for the morning.
⁷O Israel, put your hope in the Lord,
    for with the Lord is unfailing love
    and with him is full redemption.
⁸He himself will redeem Israel
    from all their sins.

We might assume that with an opening sentence, 'Out of the depths I cry to you, O Lord', this Psalm would be regularly used at a funeral. It would seem to be an ideal expression of where many of us feel we are on such an occasion. As one of only four Psalms printed in the funeral service in the Church of England *Alternative Service Book*, this is certainly the assumption. However, my experience is that it is rarely chosen. Even though there is the instruction that 'one or more of the Psalms' may be used, in practice only one is used, and 23 or 121 usually gets the vote. So this gem of a Psalm is overlooked.

There is another reason for this: the mention of 'sins' and 'forgiveness'. We realise that the depths and despair of the Psalmist are not caused primarily by factors such as illness, pain, loneliness, but by an awareness of what his life looks like to God, of his desperate need of mercy and forgiveness. It is a symptom of this human predicament that we often prefer to ignore it. Yet it is the heart of the matter of our relationship with God and of our readiness to stand before him as our judge. The Psalm expresses the realisation that 'If you, O Lord, kept a record of sins, who could stand?'; it is the unpalatable but often repeated insights of the biblical writers that we are unworthy to stand in the Lord's presence. However, this is not the end of the story. From verse 4 onwards there is a hope in God, despite all the failure, because with him 'there is forgiveness' and 'unfailing love' (v. 7).

This healthy spiritual realism prevents us either from assuming that God has no standards or justice, or from painting the deceased as someone without fault or 'sin' who has never done anything wrong. The Psalm helps us to face both the problem of our unworthiness and the solution in God's mercy and forgiveness. It can give us a firm basis of hope for the deceased, and for ourselves who one day will also stand before the Lord.

Psalm 103

8The Lord is compassionate and gracious,
    slow to anger, abounding in love.
9He will not always accuse,
    nor will he harbour his anger for ever;
10he does not treat us as our sins deserve
    or repay us according to our iniquities.
11For as high as the heavens are above the earth,
    so great is his love for those who fear him;

12as far as the east is from the west,
    so far has he removed our transgressions from us.
13As a father has compassion on his children,
    so the Lord has compassion on those who fear him;
14for he knows how we are formed,
    he remembers that we are dust.
15As for man, his days are like grass,
    he flourishes like a flower of the field;
16the wind blows over it and it is gone,
    and its place remembers it no more.
17But from everlasting to everlasting
    the Lord's love is with those who fear him,
    and his righteousness with their children's children –
18with those who keep his covenant
    and remember to obey his precepts.

Some services suggest this Psalm as an alternative at this point in the service; the modern Church of England service places these verses just before the words of committal, but omits verses 9 to 12 – rather unfortunately, in the light of the comments above on Psalm 130. It would seem enormously encouraging to realise that, because of his great love (v. 11), God does not deal with us 'as our sins deserve'; instead he deals with the sins, removing them completely from the reckoning (v. 12). How he has done this is not explained here; Christians believe it was achieved through his intervention in Christ, who 'died for sins once and for all, the righteous for the unrighteous' (1 Peter 3:18).

These verses also (as in Psalm 90) dare to articulate our mortality, the brevity and vulnerability of life (vv. 14–16). The Psalmist dares to speak in this way because he knows the answer is in the fatherly compassion of God (v. 12) and his everlasting love (v. 17).

There is something very reassuring when these verses are used, particularly at the committal of an older member of a family; the Lord's love will continue down the generations (v. 17). Children and grandchildren may have less awareness of the reality of God, but he is equally accessible and approachable for them.

Hymn: 'Praise, my soul, the King of heaven'

Praise, my soul, the King of heaven;
To His feet thy tribute bring,
Ransomed, healed, restored, forgiven,
Who like thee His praise should sing?
Praise Him! Praise Him! Praise Him! Praise Him!
Praise the everlasting King.

Praise Him for His grace and favour
To our fathers in distress;
Praise Him, still the same for ever,
Slow to chide and swift to bless.
Praise Him! Praise Him! Praise Him! Praise Him!
Glorious in His faithfulness.

Father-like, He tends and spares us;
Well our feeble frame He knows;
In His hands He gently bears us,
Rescues us from all our foes.
Praise Him! Praise Him! Praise Him! Praise Him!
Widely as His mercy flows.

Frail as summer's flower we flourish,
Blows the wind, and it is gone;
But while mortals rise and perish
God endures unchanging on:
Praise Him! Praise Him! Praise Him! Praise Him!
Praise the high Eternal One.

Angels, help us to adore Him;
Ye behold Him face to face;
Sun and moon, bow down before Him,
Dwellers all in time and space.
Praise Him! Praise Him! Praise Him! Praise Him!
Praise with us the God of grace.

It is not always realised that this is a paraphrase of Psalm 103. Of course it is often chosen to be sung near the start of the funeral as a great hymn of praise in its own right, centring our thoughts on God, rather than chosen because it is a version of one of the possible Psalms. As with 'Crimond' it is frequently used because it is so well known and perhaps was sung at earlier family occasions, for example when the deceased was married. The writer of the hymn, Henry Francis Lyte, was an Anglican clergyman in the first half of the nineteenth century. His other very famous hymn is 'Abide with me'.

The hymn begins with personal praise for all that the Lord has done for us. The Psalmist wrote 'praise the Lord, O my soul, and forget not all his benefits' and in the hymn four benefits are referred to: 'ransomed, healed, restored, forgiven'. It may seem that the mention of healing is out of place in a funeral, especially when the death has followed a long or painful illness and when many prayers had been offered for healing and recovery. Whatever the experience of the Psalmist, which prompted the writing of this Psalm, we do not always know the healing of physical or emotional illness. Forgiveness from God is guaranteed to all who call on him, but not healing. When it comes, we rejoice in it, but we know that eventually our bodies will fail and so we look forward to that fuller healing and restoration beyond this life. As we sing the verse, perhaps we can reflect that only the dead enjoy in full measure the benefits referred to.

Verses 2 to 4 of the hymn correspond to the section of the Psalm most often used at funerals, 'Slow to chide and swift to bless' is a wonderful summary of verses 8 to 12, and verses 13 to 14 are beautifully expressed in the third stanza, 'Father-like . . .'. Many hymn books omit the next stanza of the hymn which reflects the meaning of verses 15 to 17; an unfortunate omission perhaps at a funeral when the themes of our mortality and God's eternal love for us need to be expressed. It is worth including if a special service sheet is printed for the occasion.

At the end, the hymn (as the Psalm) has moved from personal praise to the adoration of God by the whole creation. In our individual funeral service we are reminded of the 'dwellers all in time and space' who praise God with us.

Alternative Psalms

A number of other Psalms are listed in the various services and, if you are responsible for preparing a service, you may like to read through some of these, in case one or more seem particularly appropriate. For example:

Psalm 27: 'The Lord is my light and my salvation – whom shall I fear?'

Psalm 42: 'As the deer pants for streams of water, so my soul pants for you, O God'.

Psalm 139: 'O Lord, you have searched me and you know me. You know when I sit and when I rise; you perceive my thoughts from afar'.

CHAPTER 4

❧ Listening to God's Word
Readings

ONE OR MORE readings from the New Testament are at
the heart of nearly every Christian funeral service. Even if a Psalm
is sung or said, there needs also to be at least one passage of Scripture which focuses on Jesus Christ and on the faith of his early followers. (Where the funeral is in the setting of a Holy Communion
or Mass, there is always a gospel reading in addition to others from
the Old and New Testaments.)

Here is the proclamation and announcement of the Christian hope. It undergirds all that is said and done in the rest of the
service. It will usually be referred to and explained in the ser-
mon/address which follows. It will provide the firm basis and context for the prayers and the committal – and then for the way in
which the bereaved will continue to cope with their grief and with
life.

This may be the first point in the service at which the congregation sits. Now is the time to receive encouragement from
God, to listen to what Christians describe as 'the Word of the
Lord'. If the opening sentences of Scripture were like headlines,
then here is the news, the Good News, in greater detail. Through
the reading of the words of Jesus Christ or of his apostles we are
reminded that death is not the end and we have the strongest reasons for holding on to the hope of eternal life. Such hope is not
wishful thinking or the mouthing of vague platitudes. It genuinely lifts our eyes to heaven because it is earthed in what God has
said and done through Jesus, particularly his crucifixion and resurrection.

47

So, we prepare to hear 'the Word of the Lord'. The Lord has a message which will help many to make some sense of what has happened. Furthermore, even as the same passage is heard by all, some can experience the Lord speaking personally to them through a word or phrase, perhaps triggering thoughts or memories, perhaps enabling them to draw new strength and comfort from it.

Preparation for this section of the service may have included beforehand the choice of a passage and of someone, other than the minister, to read it. Now at this point in the service, the congregation can be helped to prepare to listen. The minister may give a brief introduction to the passage. In the United Reformed Church service, there is a choice of prayers here which ask for God to 'speak to us once more your joyful message' and for us 'to listen lovingly for your Word'.

In this chapter we shall look at the three readings printed in the modern Church of England service and at some of the other readings suggested in that and other services.

Finally we shall consider three of the most popular non-scriptural readings which people request. These are not to be regarded as alternatives to a reading from the New Testament, but could be used at some other place in the service – perhaps as part of the sermon or within the section of prayers. The Christian funeral service must focus on Jesus Christ, and on the message from him and concerning him. There is an incident recorded in the sixth chapter of John's gospel when some people who had been following Jesus decided to leave, and Jesus asked his immediate group of twelve if they would do the same. Peter's reply was: 'Lord, to whom shall we go? You have the words of eternal life.' That same faith explains the significance of the New Testament reading in the funeral service .

John 14:1–6

[1]'Do not let your hearts be troubled. Trust in God; trust also in me. [2]In my Father's house are many rooms; if it were

not so, I would have told you. I am going there to prepare a place for you. ³And if I go and prepare a place for you, I will come back and take you to be with me that you also may be where I am. ⁴You know the way to the place where I am going.'

⁵Thomas said to him, 'Lord, we don't know where you are going, so how can we know the way?'

⁶Jesus answered, 'I am the way and the truth and the life. No-one comes to the Father except through me.'

I guess this is the passage most often chosen to be read. It has a directness and an immediacy; the words of Jesus were addressed to his disciples, but we hear them as if spoken to us. They meet us where we are, our hearts are troubled, and they describe in simple terms a heaven which most of us long for, for ourselves and for those who have died.

The description of heaven as a house, where we shall be 'at home' is very attractive, and evocative. Most of us have the experience of longing for home when far away, or of welcoming home family or friends after a long absence. There is no shortage of space in heaven in 'many rooms'. The old translation was 'many mansions' which always seemed illogical, if they were within one house! However the other meaning of 'my Father's house' in the gospels was the Temple in Jerusalem where there were rooms and apartments for many, as well as the areas for worship. So, something more spacious than the rooms of a semi-detached is indicated.

However, the newer translation 'rooms' could mislead us as much as 'mansions'. The emphasis is not on the size or separateness of individual accommodation. The original word means places we can stay, remaining there permanently with the Lord. Jesus' teaching is not about the number or size of rooms, but about there being room in heaven – room for ever, and room for many. There is no danger of the 'Full' sign suddenly going up! Religious groups have a distressing tendency to limit the accommodation in heaven, usually to themselves. The best-known example is that of the Jehovah's Witnesses, taking the symbolic number of 144,000 in the book of Revelation as the literal total of those who will have a place in the presence of God. However, this number is merely a symbol of the whole company of God's people, and in the same chapter we read the description of 'a great multitude that no-one could count, from every nation, tribe, people, and language, standing before the throne' (Revelation 7:9).

In a lighter vein, Christian groups sometimes tell the following story against themselves (or others). St Peter was showing a number of new arrivals around heaven. They came to an area where they could hear voices behind a high wall. 'Walk very quietly here', said St Peter. 'These are the Anglicans / Catholics / charismatics . . . (there are various options according to who is telling it) and they think they are the only people here.'

As we mentioned in the Postscript to Chapter 2, Christians do not necessarily believe that all will go to heaven, but there is certainly room for all who want to enjoy the presence of God and the fullness of life he 'has prepared for those who love him' (St Paul in 1 Corinthians 2:9, quoting Isaiah 64:4).

In verses 2 and 3 of John chapter 14, Jesus refers to this task of preparing a place for us. He goes ahead of us, facing death and overcoming it, so that there can be room, even for undeserving people like us. The picture is far more than that of the loving and considerate way in which family or friends may work hard to make it possible for us to arrive and feel immediately welcome and 'at home'. The preparation involved suffering and crucifixion, and then resurrection. So Jesus made a way, indeed *is* 'the way', by which we can come into relationship with God the Father in this life and dwell in his 'house' in eternity.

Finally, what do we make of the words of Jesus (in verse 3) of returning to take us to be with him? Probably the primary reference is to what Christians call the Return or the Second Coming of Christ at the end of history, the end of time; an event also mentioned in the next two passages in this chapter (1 Corinthians 15 and 1 Thessalonians 4). That return of Christ will bring history to its conclusion and fulfilment, and it will result in all God's people entering together into the resurrection life of heaven.

However, it also seems valid to see a reference to the Easter story and Jesus' 'Return' to his disciples, appearing to them over a period of forty days, to show he was really alive beyond death. As a consequence, the living Jesus Christ is the companion of his disciples then and now, and through his Spirit he takes us through this life until the time we go to be with him. This companionship will include for some people a deep sense of the presence of Christ in the final days and moments of life. Even where there is not this personal awareness, the Christian can still believe in the promise of Christ to be present then, as throughout our lives, and to take us personally across 'the narrow stream of death'.

'Trust also in me' (v. 1). The promises in this stirring passage are not empty words. The Christian believes that, especially in the light of the cross and resurrection, here is someone who can be completely trusted.

1 Corinthians 15:20–58

20But Christ has indeed been raised from the dead, the firstfruits of those who have fallen asleep. 21For since death came through a man, the resurrection of the dead comes also through a man. 22For as in Adam all die, so in Christ all will be made alive. 23But each in his own turn: Christ, the firstfruits; then, when he comes, those who belong to him. 24Then the end will come, when he hands over the kingdom to God the Father after he has destroyed all dominion, authority and power. 25For he must reign until he has put all his enemies under his feet. 26The last enemy to be destroyed is death. 27For he 'has put everything under his feet'. Now when it says that 'everything' has been put under him, it is clear that this does not include God himself, who put everything under Christ. 28When he has done this, then the Son himself will be made subject to him who put everything under him, so that God may be all in all.

29Now if there is no resurrection, what will those do who are baptised for the dead? If the dead are not raised at all, why are people baptised for them? 30And as for us, why do we endanger ourselves every hour? 31I die every day – I mean that, brothers – just as surely as I glory over you in Christ Jesus our Lord. 32If I fought wild beasts in Ephesus for merely human reasons, what have I gained? If the dead are not raised,

'Let us eat and drink,
    for tomorrow we die.'

33Do not be misled: 'Bad company corrupts good character.' 34Come back to your senses as you ought, and stop sinning; for there are some who are ignorant of God – I say this to your shame.

35But someone may ask, 'How are the dead raised? With what kind of body will they come?' 36How foolish! What you sow does not come to life unless it dies. 37When you sow, you do not plant the body that will be, but just a seed, perhaps of wheat or of something else. 38But God gives it a body as he has determined, and to each kind of seed he gives its own body. 39All flesh is not the same: Men have one kind of flesh, animals have another, birds another and fish another. 40There are also heavenly bodies and there are earthly bodies; but the splendour of the heavenly bodies is one kind, and the splendour of the earthly bodies is another. 41The sun has one kind of splendour, the moon another and the stars another; and star differs from star in splendour.

42So will it be with the resurrection of the dead. The body that is sown is perishable, it is raised imperishable; 43it is sown in dishonour, it is raised in glory; it is sown in weakness, it is raised in power; 44it is sown a natural body, it is raised a spiritual body.

If there is a natural body, there is also a spiritual body. 45So it is written: 'The first man Adam became a living being'; the last Adam, a life-giving spirit. [46]The spiritual did not come first, but the natural, and after that the spiritual. [47]The first man was of the dust of the earth, the second man from heaven. [48]As was the earthly man, so are those who are of the earth; and as is the man from heaven, so also are those who are of heaven. [49]And just as we have borne the likeness of the earthly man, so shall we bear the likeness of the man from heaven.

[50]I declare to you, brothers, that flesh and blood cannot inherit the kingdom of God, nor does the perishable inherit the imperishable. [51]Listen, I tell you a mystery: We will not all sleep, but we will all be changed – [52]in a flash, in the twinkling of an eye, at the last trumpet. For the trumpet will sound, the dead will be raised imperishable, and we will be changed. [53]For the perishable must clothe itself with the imperishable, and the mortal with immortality. [54]When the perishable has been clothed with the imperishable, and the mortal with immortality, then the saying that is written will come true: 'Death has been swallowed up in victory.'

[55]'Where, O death, is your victory?
Where, O death, is your sting?'

[56]The sting of death is sin, and the power of sin is the law. [57]But thanks be to God! He gives us the victory through our Lord Jesus Christ.

[58]Therefore, my dear brothers, stand firm. Let nothing move you. Always give yourselves fully to the work of the Lord, because you know that your labour in the Lord is not in vain.

In the traditional *Book of Common Prayer*, the only lesson for the funeral service was this long reading from verse 20 right through to the end. Most modern services include the chapter as one of the options, usually with a more limited selection of verses. For example, the Church of England's modern service prints verses

20–6, 35–8, 42–4, 53–8. It is the great chapter in the Bible on the doctrine of the resurrection. The basis of this belief, as Paul argues earlier in chapter 15, is in the fact of Christ's own resurrection and therefore one could argue that the Easter story at the end of the four gospels constitutes the obvious starting point for thinking through the belief. (And of course for so many people the Easter story opens the way to believe not only in the resurrection of the body but in Jesus Christ as truly God living a human life.) However, this chapter in the first letter to the church at Corinth is a systematic treatment of the subject, presumably because some of its members had great problems with it.

It seems from the paragraph prior to where our reading starts that some were ruling out any idea of resurrection on principle. Their 'philosophy' emphasised the importance of the soul or spirit rather than the body; death meant escape from the body and any future existence was in terms of the immortality of the soul. However the Jewish and biblical view is of human beings created by God as soul and body. The physical and the material really matter. This is underlined for Christians by the 'incarnation' of Jesus Christ: the belief that he came to live a real human life from the womb onwards. Incarnation means taking on our flesh, sharing our physical and bodily existence. Therefore, our future life, when we shall be more fully human, will continue to involve soul and body, even if it is a different kind of body, as Paul says later in the chapter.

Paul confronts the philosophical doubts about the idea of resurrection, shared by many today, by making two main points in the first nineteen verses. First, the fact of Christ's resurrection. After he was raised from death, many people saw him, including five hundred at the same time; most of whom, he adds, are still alive and therefore could verify what he says. Second, the resurrection is central to the Christian faith, and the whole thing really falls to the ground without it.

Our reading starts with Paul's confident affirmation of Christ's resurrection and of ours. His resurrection is the *guarantee* of ours. Paul twice uses the illustration of 'first fruits', which

point to a greater harvest which will come later. Death is an
'enemy', but because Christ has overcome it, it will eventually 'be
destroyed', and there will be life for all 'who belong to Christ'.

In the next paragraph, Paul explains that Christ's own resurrection body is the *model* of ours. Of course it is impossible to
understand fully or describe in any detail what our future life will
be like. However, this does not deny its reality. The illustration
of the seed and the wheat highlights the differences in appearance
before and after 'death', even though there is also a continuity.
Modern preachers often use the illustration of the caterpillar and
butterfly to make the same kind of point. However the main key
to our understanding is what we know of Jesus' appearance after
the resurrection. There was continuity: he was recognised by his
followers, although not always immediately because of the unex-
pectedness, the shock of his coming to them. There were also differences: he was no longer subject to the limits of space and time.
Unfortunately, the verses from 1 Corinthians 15, as printed in
most service books, do not include verse 49: 'And just as we have
borne the likeness of the earthly man, so shall we bear the likeness
of the man from heaven.' This most clearly spells out that Christ's
body after the resurrection is the model for ours. Even so Paul's
words (vv. 42–4) about the body which is sown and the one which
is raised (imperishable, in glory, etc.) are based on that idea of
Christ as the prototype.

Near the end of the chapter, Paul assures his readers that
Christ's resurrection victory is the *assurance* of our victory over
death. As we look at verses 55 to 57, we realise that victory does not
equal survival. 'The sting of death is sin.' In other words the problem is not that death might mean the end of the line, after which we
cease to exist, but that it will lead us into the presence of a God
before whom we are unworthy to stand. The real sting which has
to be drawn is 'sin', our failure to be the kind of people we should
be, and the 'law' of God only highlights that failure. How can we
stand before God? How can we be able to live with him for ever?

Here we are into the concepts of justice and judgment,
which we nearly all agree with as necessary for this life and indeed

in an after-life; we want evil to be punished and wrongs to be righted. However, we don't want the concepts to apply to us, and hope or assume we are exempt!

Christians do not believe God becomes unjust or suspends judgment. They do believe however that when 'Christ died for our sins' (v. 3 of this chapter), he was in a sense facing the judgment of sin which we deserved. God was in Christ not turning a blind eye to sin, but facing up to what it is and to what it does to the all-important relationship between God and the people he created. The resurrection proves that what Christ did on the cross was real. It opens the way for us to be acquitted and forgiven, and to enjoy the fellowship of a perfect and holy God here and in eternity. The sting of death has been drawn. It was a real victory, and one in which we can share.

Finally, the resurrection of Christ is the strong *motivation* for our life and work now (v. 58). There are always a few fanatics who get obsessed by the end of the world and ignore their responsibilities in this life. Perhaps even more will appear as we approach the end of the millennium! However, the Christian hope should give a new stability, and a new resolve to serve God. A belief in resurrection should result in a clearer sense of purpose in all we do in this life.

1 Thessalonians 4:13–18

13Brothers, we do not want you to be ignorant about those who fall asleep, or to grieve like the rest of men, who have no hope. 14We believe that Jesus died and rose again and so we believe that God will bring with Jesus those who have fallen asleep in him. 15According to the Lord's own word, we tell you that we who are still alive, who are left till the coming of the Lord, will certainly not precede those who have fallen asleep. 16For the Lord himself will come down from heaven, with a loud command, with the voice of the archangel and with the trumpet call of God, and the dead in Christ will rise first. 17After that, we who are still alive and are left will be caught up together with them in the clouds to meet the Lord in the air. And so we will be with the Lord for ever. [18]Therefore encourage each other with these words.

This is the reading I have used most often in funeral services down the years, but I realise that its context and the problems of the original readers are rather different from our own. This is probably the first of St Paul's letters which has survived, which would make it the earliest New Testament book. In those early years, the expectation of the return of Christ (still today part of the Christian creeds) was at the forefront of their thinking. Several were surprised that some of their fellow-Christians had died before that great event, and wondered if in some way they would miss out on the excitement and the benefits of meeting the Lord on that day. So, for them, the return was expected, and death seemed unlikely. For us, it is usually the other way round!

However, the truth of the Christian hope, which Paul spells out in striking and memorable language, still holds good. What we probably find most strange are the details (in verses 16 and 17) of what the coming of the Lord will be like. Admittedly, the details are few, because the aim is not to satisfy people's curiosity but to help their living and their grieving. Yet they can jar, and it is important to regard them as symbolic and poetic rather than a literal programme of events on the Last Day.

Now some comments on a few of the key phrases in the passage.

'Those who have fallen asleep.' Christianity is not the only religion to describe death as 'sleep', but it is a particularly appropriate word in the Christian context; death is overcome and is certainly not the end. Christians are divided over whether the 'time' between the individual's death and the resurrection of all God's people (if 'time' has any meaning at all when we are with the Lord in eternity) is one of unconsciousness and sleep. It seems that we are immediately in the presence of the Lord. Jesus says to the persistent thief 'Today you will be with me in paradise' (Luke 23:43), and Paul describes death as going to 'be with Christ which is far better' (Philippians 1:23). Personally I find it hard to believe that we shall not be aware of the Lord's presence, and I therefore tend to regard 'sleep' just as a metaphor of death.

'Not to grieve.' Many commentators highlight the contrast between the early church and the pagan systems of thought in their approach and attitudes to death. Christians had a confident and glorious hope. Surely a hope does not protect us from the natural human grief caused by separation and bereavement, but this grief is not like those who have no hope. The balance of grief and hope is important to maintain. Many of us may deny ourselves the opportunity to grieve, but often for cultural rather than Christian reasons. However, we must not lose the sense of hope. The whole funeral service is full of this 'sure and certain hope'. Passages like this indeed give us something with which to 'encourage (comfort) one another' (v. 18).

'Together with them.' Heaven will be a place of reunion, of meeting again those who have died before or after us. It is a very comforting thought for those who have been bereaved. The possibility of recognition, communicating and relating is of course made possible by the resurrection of our bodies. This may pose problems in our minds when we think of those we know only as young children, or very elderly or seriously ill or handicapped. I don't think it is fanciful to believe that in God's new creation our resurrection bodies will perfectly express the heart and the potential of all that we are, and also that we shall recognise each other immediately – and joyfully.

Presumably, heaven will also give the opportunity to forgive, explain, understand; we do not always live with others, or part from them, on good terms. There will be some people we are anxious about meeting again! But we shall be so much better equipped to meet and relate, because God will be completing his work of conforming us 'to the likeness of his Son' (Romans 8:29). St John puts it like this: 'When he appears, we shall be like him, for we shall see him as he is' (1 John 3:2).

'With the Lord for ever.' In this phrase, Paul expresses the

heart of the Christian hope, and the key fact about heaven (see the Postscript at the end of this chapter). Even more wonderful for the Christian than the hope of being together with others is the complete security of God's presence. Paul wrote this section because of the Thessalonians' anxiety about some of their friends who had died; this was the most reassuring statement he could have made to set their hearts at rest.

John 6:35-40

35Then Jesus declared, 'I am the bread of life. He who comes to me will never go hungry, and he who believes in me will never be thirsty. 36But as I told you, you have seen me and still you do not believe. 37All that the Father gives me will come to me, and whoever comes to me I will never drive away. 38For I have come down from heaven not to do my will but to do the will of him who sent me. 39And this is the will of him who sent me, that I shall lose none of all that he has given me, but raise them up at the last day. 40For my Father's will is that everyone who looks to the Son and believes in him shall have eternal life, and I will raise him up at the last day.'

This is one of the alternative readings suggested in the Church of England's modern service. Part of the passage (vv. 37–40) is printed in the funeral services book used at many crematoria and cemeteries, within the form of service produced by the Joint Liturgical Group. On the assumption that it is helpful for most people to be able to follow the reading, this makes the passage a real option in such chapels. (This also applies to the readings from Romans 8, Romans 14, and Revelation 21/22 considered later in this chapter.)

These few verses are part of a long section of teaching by Jesus, in which he builds on the people's recent experience of the miraculous feeding of five thousand with a few loaves and fishes; hence his description of himself as 'The bread of life'. The paragraph has a direction and authority because it consists of Jesus' own words. As the translation above suggests, it is a bold *declaration*.

Jesus has many striking things to say about himself and his work. He came down from heaven, God the Father's plan for people revolves around them coming to Jesus, and he is the source of their life and their eventual resurrection.

In the setting of a funeral, Jesus' promises have an obvious relevance:

- the promise of *welcome* and *security*. Those who come to him (that is, by responding to him and believing in him) will never be rejected, No one is too bad to receive a welcome which expresses complete pardon and restoration. And once people belong to him, he will keep them safe, even through death.
- the promise of *eternal life*. This is for now, as well as after death. That is why Jesus speaks (in verse 35) of our needs being met, our longings fulfilled, through coming to him. It would be valid to hear verse 35 as his encouragement to us in our grieving to turn to him with our sense of emptiness and loneliness. In heaven we shall experience more completely, but not for the first time, the quality of life which comes from belonging to God.
- the promise of *resurrection*. 'I will raise him up at the last day' is a kind of refrain in this chapter, occurring twice in this paragraph, and twice in later verses. Jesus wants us to get the message!

John 11:17–27

17On his arrival, Jesus found that Lazarus had already been in the tomb for four days. 18Bethany was less than two miles from Jerusalem, 19and many Jews had come to Martha and Mary to comfort them in the loss of their brother. 20When Martha heard that Jesus was coming, she went out to meet him, but Mary stayed at home.

21'Lord,' Martha said to Jesus, 'if you had been here, my brother would not have died. 22But I know that even now God will give you whatever you ask.'

23Jesus said to her, 'Your brother will rise again.'

24Martha answered, 'I know he will rise again in the resurrection at the last day.'

25Jesus said to her, 'I am the resurrection and the life. He who believes in me will live, even though he dies; 26and whoever lives and believes in me will never die. Do you believe this?'

27'Yes, Lord,' she told him, 'I believe that you are the Christ, the Son of God, who was to come into the world.'

We have already commented on this passage in Chapter 2 (page 19) because Jesus' declaration in verses 25 to 26 is regularly used as the first 'sentence of Scripture' at the start of the service.

This reading gives the context for those marvellous words. it is a situation which may mirror our own: the family coping with loss, the questions which inevitably come to our minds (v. 21), but also our faith in the middle of it all (v. 27).

Romans 8:31–9

31What, then, shall we say in response to this? If God is for us, who can be against us? 32He who did not spare his own Son, but gave him up for us all – how will he not also, along with him, graciously give us all things? 33Who will bring any charge against those whom God has chosen? It is God who justifies. 34Who is he that condemns? Christ Jesus, who died – more than that, who was raised to life – is at the right hand of God and is also interceding for us. 35Who shall separate us from the love of Christ? Shall trouble or hardship or persecution or famine or nakedness or danger or sword? 36As it is written:

'For your sake we face death all day long;
we are considered as sheep to be slaughtered.'

37No, in all these things we are more than conquerors through him who loved us. 38For I am convinced that neither death nor life, neither angels nor demons, neither the present nor the future, nor any powers, 39neither height nor depth, nor anything else in all creation, will be able to separate us from the love of God that is in Christ Jesus our Lord.

In the Church of England *Alternative Service Book 1980* this passage is printed as part of a service which may be used before a funeral – either in the home, or if the body is brought to church the day before (see Chapter 11). This means that, if it is chosen as the funeral reading for a service in church, there may be books or booklets available in which to follow the passage.

This is one of the most encouraging and stirring passages in the New Testament. It is not hard to see why it is often chosen for a funeral, particularly where the dead person and/or the family have a strong Christian faith. The verses refer to so many of the key beliefs; this is because St Paul is spelling out the exciting conclusions of all that he has written in the letter so far about God's work of bringing salvation and life to people through Jesus Christ. What a climax!

Sometimes I think of the passage being like a rich meal which needs to be taken slowly, in small mouthfuls, savouring and appreciating it at leisure. That may be possible in a Bible study group or in an individual's personal reading of the Bible, but hardly in the middle of a funeral service. Therefore, it may be helpful to think of it as a majestic river, flowing along with great power and beauty, and carrying us along with it.

However, notice en route the five questions which do not get or need an answer. The answers are obvious in the light of what Paul writes:

Verse 31: nothing we face can prevail or overcome us, because God is 'for us', committed to our well-being for all eternity.

Verse 32: of course he will give us all we need; the cross is the guarantee of his generous love.

Verse 33: no charge can stick if we belong to a pardoning, forgiving God.

Verse 34: one day we will face the scrutiny of God and give account to him of our lives (see the next reading from Romans 14), but those who trust in the mercy of God in Christ will never be condemned.

Verse 35: nothing can separate us, not even the most terrible circumstances. St Paul turns the question into a declaration in the great climax of verses 38 to 39. Nothing can separate us from God's love; certainly not death.

Sometimes when I have read this passage at a funeral, a few people have responded with an audible 'Amen'! In some cases this may have been a reflex action because the final words 'in Christ Jesus our Lord' also conclude many prayers which then require an 'Amen'. However, here is a passage which so stirs and moves us that it almost demands a joyful response.

Romans 14:7–12

7For none of us lives to himself alone and none of us dies to himself alone. 8If we live, we live to the Lord; and if we die, we die to the Lord. So, whether we live or die, we belong to the Lord.

9For this very reason, Christ died and returned to life so that he might be the Lord of both the dead and the living. 10You, then, why do you judge your brother? Or why do you look down on your brother? For we will all stand before God's judgment seat. 11It is written:

'As surely as I live,' says the Lord,
'Every knee will bow before me;
　　every tongue will confess to God.'

12So then, each of us will give an account of himself to God.

The modern Church of England service suggests that only verses 7 to 9 are read. However, verses 10 to 12 give us a reminder of the context of this passage, and also introduce the theme of the last judgment – which we may not want to hear about, but that is hardly a valid reason for ignoring it!

In this chapter, Paul is addressing divisions in the church at Rome. The issue is not a major doctrinal theme, but seems to be the much more secondary matter of what Christians should eat or drink. Some believers felt able to disregard the food laws of the Old Testament as no longer applying to them, but they then looked down on those who came to a different conclusion. In turn, this second group were apt to judge the others for being law-breakers. Paul's view is that, in a minor matter like this, mutual love and respect are more important than the rights and wrongs of the case.

Therefore, let us remember that when we stand before God, each of us shall give an account of our own life, not of anyone else's (v. 12). For Christians, the fact of a 'last judgment' does not negate the assurance of all sins forgiven because of the death of Jesus Christ; it does however remind them of their responsibility to live and act as before God and in his presence.

This links with verses 7 and 8. Whatever the different decisions we make about matters of behaviour, the principle is that of serving and pleasing Christ; and the principle holds good not only in life, but in death – the way we die, entrusting ourselves to the Lord, and after death, as our service continues.

So to the great affirmations by Paul, which make the reading so appropriate at a funeral. Before and after death we belong to the Lord (v. 8), and this is possible because Christ himself went through death to the resurrection life beyond (v. 9).

2 Corinthians 4:7–18

7But we have this treasure in jars of clay to show that this all-surpassing power is from God and not from us. 8We are hard pressed on every side, but not crushed; perplexed, but not in despair; [9]persecuted, but not abandoned; struck down, but not destroyed. [10]We always carry around in our body the death of Jesus, so that the life of Jesus may also be revealed in our body. [11]For we who are alive are always being given over to death for Jesus' sake, so that his life may be revealed in our mortal body. [12]So then, death is at work in us, but life is at work in you.

[13]It is written: 'I believed; therefore I have spoken.' With that same spirit of faith we also believe and therefore speak, [14]because we know that the one who raised the Lord Jesus from the dead will also raise us with Jesus and present us with you in his presence. [15]All this is for your benefit, so that the grace that is reaching more and more people may cause thanksgiving to overflow to the glory of God.

[16]Therefore we do not lose heart. Though outwardly we are wasting away, yet inwardly we are being renewed day by day. [17]For our light and momentary troubles are achieving for us an eternal glory that far outweighs them all. [18]So we fix our eyes not on what is seen, but on what is unseen. For what is seen is temporary, but what is unseen is eternal.

This rich and, in places, complicated reading wonderfully reaffirms the heart of the Christian Good News, a message of life and hope. However, as always in the New Testament, the message is not one of escape from, or immunity to, the turmoil and troubles of life. Rather, the Christian faith and hope carry us through such times.

At a funeral, we relate to Paul's experience of being 'hard-pressed' and 'perplexed'. However, his experience is also one of knowing God's power, his strong help, so that he is not crushed or in despair. This service encourages us to find that same help. The circumstances are indeed difficult, but that is not the end of the story. We can know the living Jesus Christ with us and in us (vv. 10 and 11).

I appreciate verse 16 more as I get older and as more parts

of me don't seem to work properly! Whatever is happening to me 'outwardly' and physically, Christ's life is gradually renewing and transforming the kind of person I am.

Beyond this life is the 'eternal glory' (v. 17), and our sure grasp on such a hope helps to put this life's troubles and suffering in context. 'Light and momentary troubles' is not a denial of what we go through, but an appreciation of how we can view them in the light of eternity. Paul puts it like this in his letter to the Romans: 'I consider that our present sufferings are not worth comparing with the glory that will be revealed in us' (Romans 8:18). So the reading finishes with the encouragement to keep eternal truths and eternal things in our sights.

Philippians 3:10–21

10I want to know Christ and the power of his resurrection and the fellowship of sharing in his sufferings, becoming like him in his death, 11and so, somehow, to attain to the resurrection from the dead.

12Not that I have already obtained all this, or have already been made perfect, but I press on to take hold of that for which Christ Jesus took hold of me. 13Brothers, I do not consider myself yet to have taken hold of it. But one thing I do: Forgetting what is behind and straining towards what is ahead, 14I press on towards the goal to win the prize for which God has called me heavenwards in Christ Jesus.

15All of us who are mature should take such a view of things. And if on some point you think differently, that too God will make clear to you. 16Only let us live up to what we have already attained.

17Join with others in following my example, brothers, and take note of those who live according to the pattern we gave you. 18For, as I have often told you before and now say again even with tears, many live as enemies of the cross of Christ. 19Their destiny is destruction, their god is their stomach, and their glory is in their shame. Their mind is on earthly things. 20But our citizenship is in heaven. And we eagerly await a Saviour from there, the Lord Jesus Christ, 21who, by the power that enables him to bring everything under his control, will transform our lowly bodies so that they will be like his glorious body.

In my experience, this suggested reading is only occasionally used at a funeral, but it begins and ends with the theme of resurrection, and in two unusual verses (14, 20) it focuses our attention heavenward.

One of the great results of the resurrection of Christ at the first Easter is that we can know him today, alive and powerful in our world and in our own lives (v. 10). As in the 2 Corinthians 4 reading, Paul first considers the implications for this life. Christianity is not some kind of guarantee of protection from suffering; indeed to be a follower of a crucified Lord can produce extra opposition and difficulty ('sharing in his sufferings'). However, through it all, we can experience the powerful companionship of Christ.

Another great result of Easter is our own resurrection (v. 11). Here we meet a word which seems so uncharacteristic of the usually bold and confident Paul: 'somehow' or 'if possible' or 'if only' are some possible translations. It seems extraordinary that he should be suddenly uncertain about the truth he proclaims in many other places, including verse 21 of this chapter. Presumably, then, the uncertainty refers to what he may yet have to go through before he dies. In fact, in chapter 1, he faces up to the possibility of an early death, but assumes he will probably be allowed more time in which to serve the Christians at Philippi and elsewhere (Philippians 1:19–26).

Verse 21 is quoted in the committal prayer in the traditional *Book of Common Prayer*. Our present body is committed to the earth, or fire, or sea, in the sure hope of the new resurrection bodies we shall receive. As in 1 Corinthians 15, Christ's resurrection body is described as the model, the prototype of ours, which will be 'raised in glory'.

Finally, the two references to heaven. Verse 14 is not so specific; 'heavenwards' is sometimes translated 'upwards' or 'high calling'. However, it doubtless includes the life of heaven which God calls us, and provides for us, to share. Using an illustration from the athletic games, Paul describes himself as running the Christian race to the limit of his energy and effort; not because the prize is in doubt, but because God has given us such an amazing call and destiny. Heaven is our home, our city (v. 20): that's where we really belong. At that time, Philippi had the privileged status of 'a colony' of Rome. Although far from Rome itself, the Philippians were regarded as citizens of that city, and the register of citizens was kept there. So Paul is saying: 'We already belong there, we already have the citizenship, and one day we shall live there.'

Revelation 21:1–7, 22:1–5

1Then I saw a new heaven and a new earth, for the first heaven and the first earth had passed away, and there was no longer any sea. 2I saw the Holy City, the new Jerusalem, coming down out of heaven from God, prepared as a bride beautifully dressed for her husband. 3And I heard a loud voice from the throne saying, 'Now the dwelling of God is with men, and he will live with them. They will be his people, and God himself will be with them and be their God. 4He will wipe every tear from their eyes. There will be no more death or mourning or crying or pain, for the old order of things has passed away.'

5He who was seated on the throne said, 'I am making everything new!' Then he said, 'Write this down, for these words are trustworthy and true.'

6He said to me: 'It is done. I am the Alpha and the Omega, the Beginning and the End. To him who is thirsty I will give to drink without cost from the spring of the water of life. 7He who overcomes will inherit all this, and I will be his God and he will be my son.'

[1]Then the angel showed me the river of the water of life, as clear as crystal, flowing from the throne of God and of the Lamb [2]down the middle of the great street of the city. On each side of the river stood the tree of life, bearing twelve crops of fruit, yielding its fruit every month. And the leaves of the tree are for the healing of the nations. [3]No longer will there be any curse. The throne of God and of the Lamb will be in the city, and his servants will serve him. [4]They will see his face, and his name will be on their foreheads. [5]There will be no more night. They will not need the light of a lamp or the light of the sun, for the Lord God will give them light. And they will reign for ever and ever.

Usually the reading would be from just one of the chapters; most commonly from chapter 21. However some or all of these verses from both chapters may be read together. For example, 21:1–4 and 22:3–5 are printed as one reading in the crematoria service books (as part of the service prepared by the Joint Liturgical Group).

For many people, this last book of the Bible is very puzzling, with all its strange descriptions and symbolism. However, it is also a very thrilling book, written to give courage and hope to Christians in the late first century AD who were facing persecution and threat of martyrdom. The message of the book is that, whatever the power and influence of the Roman Empire, God is in control of history, he is with his people in their suffering, and he will bring them safely to glory. At the end of history God will have the last word. So the book moves towards the vision of heaven described here.

At first we are surprised that, instead of a heaven where we live with God, John has a vision of 'a new heaven and a new earth', as if God and people were at a distance. However, the distinction is left behind as we read about the future in terms of a wonderful city where God is with his people (21:3). Indeed God's throne will be there (22:3). ('The Lamb' is a common title in the book for Jesus Christ, the Son of God, who shares the throne with his Father.)

Some people would regard city life more as a picture of hell than of heaven! They resent the fact that the Bible starts in a garden (Eden) but finishes in a city. Perhaps the symbolism is necessary to indicate that the Lord makes provision for all his people – the great multitude referred to in chapter 7 of the book. However, the life of this city is far from impersonal. We shall see God (22:4), he personally will meet our needs (21:6), and we shall enjoy a family relationship with him (21:7).

Revelation 21 is often chosen as a reading simply because of verse 4. At a funeral we are so aware of death, mourning, crying and pain – certainly the emotional pain of bereavement, and perhaps also the physical pain endured by the person before their death. We are aware of all that seems to spoil life. And here is the vision, the promise, that it will not always be so. 'These words are trustworthy and true.'

In the introduction to this chapter, I referred to readings which are sometimes chosen from sources other than the Bible. Occasionally, such a choice by the family or an instruction left by the dead person, particularly if it is intended to be the only reading, can lead to some tension with the Christian minister taking the service. The minister has the responsibility to ensure the service conveys clearly the Christian message. In practice a 'compromise' can usually be reached with the non-scriptural reading being in addition to the lesson, rather than an alternative. There may be occasions when the chosen reading actually contradicts Christian belief; hopefully the minister will take time in such circumstances to point out why it would be inappropriate within a Christian funeral.

Here are three of the passages most frequently chosen, each followed by a brief comment. For a wider selection, consult the book *Funerals – A Guide: Prayers, Hymns and Readings* (details in Appendix A). There are nearly two hundred pages of passages of prose and poetry down the centuries.

'Death is nothing at all . . .'

Death is nothing at all . . . I have only slipped away into the next room. I am I and you are you. Whatever we were to each other that we are still. Call me by my old familiar name, speak to me in the easy way which you always used. Put no difference in your tone; wear no forced air of solemnity or sorrow. Laugh as we always laughed at the little jokes we enjoyed together. Play, smile, think of me, pray for me. Let my name be ever the household word that it always was. Let it be spoken without effort, without the ghost of a shadow on it. Life means all that it ever meant. It is the same as it ever was; there is absolutely unbroken continuity. Why should I be out of mind because I am out of sight? I am waiting for you for an interval, somewhere very near, just around the corner. All is well.

(Henry Scott Holland)

This passage has produced strong and conflicting reactions from Christians and others. The main debate is over the first sentence. Is death really that insignificant? For family and friends, the loss and separation are painful, at times overwhelming. For those facing death, even with strong faith in eternal life, there is inevitable apprehension, perhaps fear. It is a journey into new territory. So the passage can seem to contradict most of our feelings. Yet, for the Christian, life most certainly continues beyond death. If anything, death is a beginning rather than an ending. Scott Holland was touching on an important truth, even if there is some doubt about the way he expressed it.

After the first sentence, the passage has important things to say about coping with bereavement. This is part of a sermon preached at the time of the death of King Edward VII. I am grateful to Dr Peter Jupp for the insight that it was probably a reaction against Edwardian excesses in mourning. Particularly, it encourages a genuineness and naturalness in talking about the dead person, and in talking about them as alive still. 'Laugh' and 'smile' may seem a tall order, but I feel they have a place, even in the funeral service.

'The ship'

I am standing upon that foreshore. A ship at my side spreads her white sails in the morning breeze and starts for the blue ocean. She is an object of beauty and strength and I stand and watch her until at length she hangs like a speck of white cloud just where the sea and sky come down to mingle with each other. Then someone at my side says, 'There! She's gone!' 'Gone where?' 'Gone from my sight, that's all.' She is just as large in mast and spar and hull as ever she was when she left my side; just as able to bear her load of living freight to the place of her destination. Her diminished size is in me, not in her. And just at that moment when someone at my side says, 'There! She's gone!' there are other eyes watching her coming and other voices ready to take up the glad shout, 'Here she comes!' And that is dying.

(Victor Hugo, from *Toilers of the Sea*)

This hardly needs any comment; that's the beauty of the passage. It does not explain the basis of our trust in the new destination, such as we have in the readings from Scripture; but it is a clear reminder that the separation, the memories, the goodbyes are not the whole story.

I also see in the passage a gentle challenge to our use of various euphemisms for the dying and death. 'She's gone!' But 'Gone where?' Similarly we talk about 'Passed away' or 'Slipped away', but 'Where to?' 'He's no longer with us', but 'Where is he?' Sometimes, these little phrases seem to play down the reality of death, without emphasising the hope of life beyond.

'Footprints'

One night I had a dream.
I dreamed I was walking along the beach with the Lord,
and across the sky flashed scenes from my life.
For each scene, I noticed two sets of footprints in the sand;
one belonged to me, the other to the Lord.
When the last scene of my life flashed before me,
I looked back at the footprints in the sand.
I noticed that it happened at the very lowest and saddest
    times in my life.
This really bothered me and I questioned the Lord about
    it:
'Lord, You said that once I decided to follow You,
You would walk with me all the way.
But I have noticed that during the most troublesome
    times in my life, there is only one set of footprints.
    I don't understand why in times when I needed You
    most, You would leave me.'
The Lord replied:
'My precious, precious child, I love you and would
    never, never leave you during your times of trial and
    suffering.
When you see only one set of footprints –
It was then that I carried you.'

This is a piece of writing which seems to appear increasingly in Christian sermons, books and posters.

In this book I frequently refer to the presence of the Lord Jesus Christ with his people in their dying, their grieving, and in the rebuilding of their lives. It has to be acknowledged however that often we only fully realise this fact in retrospect. At the time it may feel a lonely struggle; we may be too dazed or shocked to appreciate the Lord's help and strengthening.

The mourners at a funeral can sense his presence through parts of the service, and through the loving support of other people, but it may be much later that they see clearly how the Lord sustained them and carried them through that part of 'the path of life'. Christians can certainly trust the words of Christ at the end of Matthew's gospel: 'I am with you always' (Matthew 28:20); even if they are not aware of him every step of the way.

POSTSCRIPT
What do we know about heaven?

Not very much, but we know enough; perhaps we are given by God as much as we can grasp this side of death. Several of the readings we have considered in this chapter help us to become aware of the main characteristics of heaven. All of them build upon what we experience in part on earth; not because heaven is merely a projection of our hopes and dreams, but because God, who gives us much to enjoy and wonder at in this life, is the same God of the new creation beyond.

God is at the centre of heaven. Living with him, in his house, as his children, is the main feature of heaven. The more we have come to enjoy a relationship with God and his Son Jesus Christ in this life, the more we look forward to what heaven is really like. As Paul wrote to the Philippian church, to go and be with Christ will be far better (Philippians 1:23). Even on earth, 'to live is Christ', and so 'to die is gain' (Philippians 1:21). Heaven will be full of the worship and praise of the Lord, and of opportunities to serve him. At last we shall be able to receive all that he has wanted to give us, and to respond to him with our whole being.

The second great characteristic of heaven is being with other people in positive and fulfilling relationships. This is where a belief in the resurrection of the body is so important; it will make possible recognition, reunion, relating. Heaven is not mere spiritual survival or some ghostly existence; it is where people meet. Nor is heaven merely about individual salvation; it is where the people, the family, the community of God share a new life together, no doubt with much joy and laughter.

I think some people are troubled by the idea of heaven as 'an eternity', which is a phrase we apply to something impossibly boring or prolonged! 'Eternity' certainly includes the meaning 'without end', but it does not describe an existence which is static, fixed or dull, but one which gives an unimaginable richness to all the best things we enjoy on earth. I do not pretend to know if we will be aware of the passage of time in heaven, or whether 'time' as such will exist there. But it seems to me that heaven must include room and scope for developing the relationships with God himself and with other people, and for enjoying and learning about the beauty with which we shall be surrounded.

It is probably impossible to visualise heaven. The pictures and descriptions in the book of Revelation are pointers to the characteristics of heaven, rather than details of what it will look like. We can happily 'wait and see'. All we know of God in this life is the guarantee that it is worth waiting for.

> My knowledge of that life is small
> The eye of faith is dim;
> But 'tis enough that Christ knows all,
> And I shall be with him.
>
> (Richard Baxter)

CHAPTER 5

❧ Words to remember
The sermon

THE 'SERMON' or 'homily' may sound a rather grand title for a talk which may last only a few minutes. Apart from the obvious time constraints, this is not an occasion for a lengthy address or detailed explanation of the Christian faith; close family and friends usually feel numb and dazed, and it is hard to concentrate on what is said. Interestingly, in the traditional *Book of Common Prayer*, there is no provision for a sermon, and in the Church of England *Alternative Service Book* it is still optional.

However, for so many people, both close mourners and other members of the congregation, the sermon can stand out in their memories when the rest of the service has been largely forgotten. Jenny Hockey carried out a survey of ministers and bereaved people in Sheffield in 1989/90 and wrote it up in *Making the Most of a Funeral*, published by Cruse-Bereavement Care. In the book, she comments, 'for many bereaved people the address is the part of the funeral which is remembered most clearly and which represents the greatest source of comfort'. The details may not stick, but the sense of genuine concern and of the reality of the Christian message can make a deep impact.

There may be the temptation to ask for the sermon to be omitted in order to make the service 'as short and simple as possible'. However this may deprive the mourners of the very ingredient in the service which can make it most personal and alive.

Although there is a natural inclination for people to hide from what has happened and from how they really feel about it, it is usually beneficial, in both the short term and long term, to be helped by the service, and especially by the sermon, to face up to things. There is the reality of death, of loss and pain, and the reminder of our own mortality. But there are also the memories of the deceased, painful to recall at such a time, but a cause for appreciation and thanksgiving. There is also the reality of the Christian Gospel, which is the Good News of God's eternal love shown in the death and resurrection of Jesus; this gives the true setting and context in which to make sense of the bereavement. Incidentally this is why 'sermon' or 'homily' is the right word; its primary aim, as in any service of worship, is to explain what has been read in the Psalms and other Scriptures (usually just prior to the sermon) and to apply them to the hearers. The funeral service in the United Reformed Church gives it the title: 'Sermon on the Christian Hope'.

One of the dilemmas for the minister, speaking at a Christian funeral service, is how to personalise it, with clear and specific references to the deceased, but at the same time putting the Christian hope clearly before people so that they are not sold short. The Roman Catholic liturgy gives the clear instruction that the homily should not be a eulogy but should be based on the readings. On the other hand, the most common complaint about a funeral is that it was impersonal, ignoring the life and sometimes even the name of the dead person.

Some ministers maintain the balance by giving a kind of 'running commentary' through the service, rather than one extended sermon slot. For example there may be some words about the deceased before the prayer of thanksgiving for their life, encouragement to the mourners before the prayers for comfort and strength, and comments after the reading(s) or perhaps as an introduction to them. Another alternative is for a relative or friend to give a separate appreciation or 'tribute', and for the minister to speak about the Christian hope – and even this could be undertaken by another suitable person able to express this message of good news. So there are various possibilities to consider in the planning even of this part of the service. And remember that if the service is to be 'personalised', it will usually depend on the minister being given the information and the details to make it so.

Not that the sermon should be a potted biography, telling people what most of them know anyway, or a eulogy in the strict sense of praising and speaking well of someone – and thereby ignoring some of the less attractive characteristics which they are well aware of! A large part of the purpose of a funeral is to help people face what really is, or was, true. Of course it is crucial to appreciate the unique personality God gave to the deceased and also the ways in which other lives have been enriched through knowing them. However, part of the picture is of failure, weakness, regrets. (I am not advocating an emphasis on the faults, but merely a real picture.)

Why is it always wrong to 'speak ill of the dead'? Partly it is because they can no longer answer back; but partly it is a feeling that we need to present their best side to God. Is this why we talk of 'praising someone to the skies'? God knows us completely anyway, and his acceptance of us is based on his mercy and forgiveness, demonstrated in Jesus Christ, and not on our record of attitude and behaviour. Christians believe he loves us as we really are. Comments such as 'She never had a harsh word to say against anyone' or 'He never did anyone any harm' are ways of expressing love and appreciation, but there is always another side to the picture, even with the best people. There needs to be a healthy reality in looking at the total picture, knowing that God looks in love on it all.

The funeral is not the place for 'revelations' of facts known only to one or two; however, it is good when difficulties which nearly everyone is aware of are not glossed over but mentioned with sensitivity. For example broken relationships and divided families may be uppermost in the thoughts of the chief mourners; some reference can help to put things in perspective and still leave room for genuine thanks for the person's life.

The heart of the sermon is the Christian Gospel. The more that people get in touch with their own feelings of loss and pain – and perhaps of anger, guilt, disappointment, bewilderment, etc. – the more they need to hear that message. The message may be set out in Psalms, hymns and readings, but it is sometimes through the more personal explanation that people find comfort and hope.

A vicar on the south coast received a letter after taking a service for a young person who had committed suicide. It included these sentences: 'I just want to say thank you for your message at Naomi's Thanksgiving. I found it really helpful the picture of God not letting go. It was important for me because twenty years ago I attempted an overdose but was found in time. I understood properly, for the first time, Romans 8.' (See Chapter 4, pages 61–2.)

It is at times of such distressing deaths, for example of a child or young person, suicide, a sudden illness or accident, that the question 'Why?' can be most urgently asked. There are no clever slick answers, but the promises of God being with us in our need and of our being with him for all eternity can help people 'hold on' when the grief seems unbearable. The best remembered and most helpful funeral talks are usually those which are straightforward and spoken with conviction and honesty; they speak to real people about the real God and his Good News.

CHAPTER 6

꧁ In tune with heaven
Hymns and other music

MUSIC HAS a vital role in a funeral service. It should contribute to the dignity and beauty of the occasion. It has the power to awaken memories, to express deep feelings, to console and to uplift the mourners.

A funeral without music is stark and impoverished. Even when there is no singing of hymns or Psalms, music can be played on the organ or other instruments, and recorded music can be used. Occasionally a funeral is taken in a cemetery chapel where no instrument is available, but a good-quality cassette recorder can make all the difference in what is often a rather dreary setting.

There is plenty of scope for choices and decisions about the funeral music, and most people have particular favourites and strong preferences. These are not always appropriate for a Christian funeral! Sometimes a hymn remembered from schooldays or from 'Songs of Praise' may be much loved and popular, but does not touch on the main themes of the service. More difficult are the choices of classical or popular music where the words contradict the Christian hope. Clearly, family and friends have the right to request hymns and other music, but the minister has the responsibility to ensure the Christian content of the service; usually some sensitive discussion can resolve any conflict.

My usual advice about the decision whether to sing at all, and then about the choice of hymns, is 'Play it safe'. Good music can transform a service, but a handful of people struggling to sing can simply be an embarrassment. The mourners may be too emotional to sing out, and the minister's voice cannot always be relied upon to give a strong lead! Obviously a choir or even a few voices can make all the difference. If it is a borderline decision, best to have familiar hymns – and perhaps only one, rather than two or three. When it is decided not to sing there is the possibility of the organ playing the hymn tune at the start or conclusion of the service.

The choice of hymns is sometimes very straightforward; the dead person has left instructions about the service or at least it is known what their favourite hymns were. Otherwise, the family may be grateful for suggestions. Thirty-eight of the most popular funeral hymns are printed in the latest edition of the 'Funeral Services' book for crematoria and cemeteries. In this chapter I suggest a 'Top Ten' and list a few others. A word of caution about tunes: several well-known hymns have a choice of tunes and it is worth checking that the organist's preference is the one you want.

Where in the service should hymns be sung? The Church of England's modern language service suggests two points: after the sermon; after the prayers and before the commendation and committal. There is particular significance in a hymn which reinforces the message of hope in the reading and sermon. At this point in the United Reformed Church service, it specifies a 'hymn of confident faith'.

In practice, hymns are commonly sung at two other places in the service: near the start, instead of a Psalm or even a matrical version of a Psalm, and near the end, where it can be appropriate to sing something quiet and meditative, or perhaps triumphant and joyful. So there are various options, but only two hymns are possible in the standard twenty minutes allowed for a service at a crematorium.

Imaginative and inspiring use can be made of other music in the service, for example a vocal or instrumental solo. I remember the impact of a trumpet solo at the funeral of a jazz enthusiast. Often the choice of music as people enter and leave the service is left to the organist, but there is a vast range of possibilities. A helpful list of appropriate recorded music can be found in *Funerals: A Guide* (see Appendix A). For church services, where people gather and sit for several minutes beforehand, the choice is particularly important. 'Jesu, joy of man's desiring', Handel's

'Largo', or 'Ave Maria' often get the vote, but there is scope for being adventurous.

Top Ten hymns

This choice is not the result of a careful survey, but of my own experience in taking funerals and talking with organists. It is still a very traditional selection, although some more modern hymns, for example 'Lord of all hopefulness', are becoming popular through school assemblies and 'Songs of Praise', and would be at least in the Top Twenty. Regular churchgoers are probably more keen to have newer hymns and songs; the only disadvantage is that a good proportion of the congregation at a funeral may be unfamiliar with them.

Only a few popular hymns were written for a funeral or on the theme of death and eternal life (e.g. 'Abide with me'). Several Easter hymns are appropriate for the service because they highlight the basis of the Christian hope (e.g. 'Thine is the glory'). Many general hymns focus on the presence of God with his people throughout life, including times of weakness and sorrow, and in death itself (e.g. 'Guide me, O thou great Redeemer').

Four of my 'Top Ten' were mentioned in Chapter 3, because they were based on Psalms: 'The Lord's my Shepherd'; 'The king of love'; 'O God, our help in ages past'; and 'Praise, my soul, the King of heaven'. In this chapter I shall comment on six other hymns, and briefly mention some others.

Hymn: 'Abide with me'

Abide with me; fast falls the eventide:
The darkness deepens; Lord, with me abide:
When other helpers fail, and comforts flee,
Help of the helpless, O abide with me.

Swift to it close ebbs out life's little day;
Earth's joys grow dim, its glories pass away;
Change and decay in all around I see:
O thou who changest not, abide with me.

I need thy presence every passing hour;
What but thy grace can foil the tempter's power?
Who like thyself my guide and stay can be?
Through cloud and sunshine, Lord, abide with me.

I fear no foe with thee at hand to bless;
Ills have no weight, and tears no bitterness.
Where is death's sting? Where, grave, thy victory?
I triumph still, if thou abide with me.

Hold thou thy cross before my closing eyes;
Shine through the gloom, and point me to the skies:
Heaven's morning breaks, and earth's vain shadows flee;
In life, in death, O Lord, abide with me.

A great hymn for a funeral! Perhaps it suffers from over-use and from its strange popularity at the Cup Final. However, I have to admit that my choice of the hymn for my father's funeral was influenced in part by the fact that he and I attended several such Cup Finals, especially when Spurs played – and usually won! It was one of the few hymns he knew well, but it is also one of the few hymns written about death and trust in God through it.

Henry Francis Lyte, who also wrote 'Praise, my soul, the King of heaven' knew he was dying when he wrote 'Abide with me'. It was completed less than three months before his death in November 1847. At first sight it may appear to be an evening hymn ('fast falls the eventide'), but in fact it refers to the evening of life ('life's little day'). The first line is virtually a quotation from a verse in Luke's gospel, chapter 24, where the risen Christ appeared to two of his disciples as they walked the seven miles from Jerusalem to a village called Emmaus on the afternoon of the first Easter Day. They had not yet recognised him, but out of cour-tesy invited him into their home because evening was approach-ing – 'stay with us, for it is nearly evening'.

Lyte turns this into our prayer to the risen Christ as we approach the evening of life or face the reality of death. We need his presence with us as we cope with the brevity of life and with the different experiences of 'cloud and sunshine', sorrow and joy. The fourth verse quotes Paul's words in 1 Corinthians 15 (see Chapter 4, pages 51–3), and does not deny the 'tears' but also proclaims the 'triumph'. The magnificent last verse speaks of heaven's new and eternal day when this life's 'little day' has ended.

Hymn: 'The day thou gavest'

The day thou gavest, Lord, is ended,
The darkness falls at thy behest;
To thee our morning hymns ascended,
Thy praise shall sanctify our rest.

We thank thee that thy church unsleeping,
While earth rolls onward into light,
Through all the world her watch is keeping,
And rests not now by day or night.

As o'er each continent and island
The dawn leads on another day,
The voice of prayer is never silent,
Nor dies the strain of praise away.

The sun that bids us rest is waking
Our friends beneath the western sky,
And hour by hour fresh lips are making
Thy wondrous doings heard on high.

So be it, Lord; thy throne shall never,
Like earth's proud empires, pass away;
Thy kingdom stands, and grows for ever,
Till all thy creatures own thy sway.

This hymn, written by John Ellerton in 1870, was chosen by Queen Victoria as one of the hymns for her

Diamond Jubilee in 1897 and has been very popular since then.

Unlike 'Abide with me' it is a true evening hymn, and its application to the evening of life is in the mind of the congregation rather than in the intention of the writer. However, it touches on several themes which are appropriate for a funeral. Each day is a gift from the Lord who controls the times and seasons. The praise of God should be the great characteristic of our days. The worldwide Church, with its constant prayer and praise throughout every 24 hours, is a pointer to God's eternal kingdom, and we look to the final day when everyone will recognise and acknowledge him.

The hymn starts with this particular day and encourages us to consider eternal things. It is the perspective we need at a funeral service.

Hymn: 'All things bright and beautiful'

All things bright and beautiful,
all creatures great and small,
all things wise and wonderful
the Lord God made them all.

Each little flower that opens,
each little bird that sings –
he made their glowing colours,
he made their tiny wings.
All things bright . . .

The purple-headed mountain,
the river running by,
the sunset, and the morning
that brightens up the sky:
All things bright . . .

wind in the winter,
asant summer sun,
pe fruits in the garden
made them every one.
All things bright . . .

He gave us eyes to see them,
and lips that we might tell
how great is God almighty,
who has made all things well!
All things bright . . .

I have mixed reactions to the apparent popularity of this hymn at funerals, not only of children but of people of all ages. Of course it was, and still is, commonly sung in school worship. Therefore it is a hymn known by nearly everyone, although there are two tunes frequently used and in choosing it you need to specify which of these you want. So, its popularity is understandable.

However, it is a hymn which does not touch on most of the great themes of a funeral service or the issues it throws up. Mrs C. F. Alexander wrote a number of hymns for children on parts of the Christian Creed: 'Once in royal David's city' and 'There is a green hill' are two of them. This hymn develops the truth 'I believe in God, the Father Almighty, Maker of heaven and earth'. Certainly, as we thank God for the dead person's life, we may recall their appreciation of nature or enjoyment of travel as well as the general sense of God providing so much in his creation for them and for us. On the other hand, I wonder if the hymn might encourage a kind of escape from the pain and sorrow of bereavement, and the need to find God's hope for the future, into the memory (or even the illusion) of a carefree childhood, or of happier and more secure days.

I understand the choice of this charming hymn but I suggest it should be balanced by another hymn (or song or Psalm) which relates more directly to how we feel and what we face.

Hymn: 'Thine be the glory'

Thine be the glory, risen, conquering Son,
Endless is the victory thou o'er death hast won;
Angels in bright raiment rolled the stone away,
Kept the folded grave-clothes where thy body lay.
Thine be the glory, risen, conquering Son,
Endless is the victory thou o'er death hast won!

Lo! Jesus meets us, risen from the tomb;
Lovingly he greets us, scatters fear and gloom;
Let the church with gladness hymns of triumph sing,
For her Lord now liveth, death hath lost its sting.
Thine be the glory, risen, conquering Son,
Endless is the victory thou o'er death hast won!

No more we doubt thee, glorious prince of life;
Life is naught without thee: aid us in our strife;
Make us more than conquerors through thy deathless love;
Bring us safe through Jordan to thy home above.
Thine be the glory, risen, conquering Son,
Endless is the victory thou o'er death hast won!

A stirring Easter hymn, usually sung to music from Handel's 'Judas Maccabaeus'. The proclamation, in the refrain, of victory over death makes it an obvious choice for a funeral.

Verse 1 recalls something of the events of the first Easter. As a result (v. 2) Jesus, who appeared to his disciples then, can meet us and transform our fear, particularly our fear of death. 'Death hath lost its sting' is based on one of the suggested funeral readings (1 Corinthians 15:55–6 – see page 53), as is 'more than conquerors' (Romans 8:37) in verse 3. This last verse expresses a bold prayer of faith that Jesus Christ will aid us in all the circumstances of life and bring us safely through death. The use of the Israelites' passage through the River Jordan into the promised land as a picture of our passing through death into

the eternal home promised to us is further developed in the next
hymn.

Hymn: 'Guide me, O thou great Redeemer'

Guide me, O thou great Redeemer,
Pilgrim through this barren land;
I am weak, but thou art mighty;
Hold me with thy powerful hand:
Bread of heaven,
Feed me now and evermore.

Open now the crystal fountain,
Whence the healing stream doth flow;
Let the fiery cloudy pillar
Lead me all my journey through:
Strong deliverer,
Be thou still my strength and shield.

When I tread the verge of Jordan,
Bid my anxious fears subside;
Death of death, and hell's destruction,
Land me safe on Canaan's side:
Songs and praises
I will ever give to thee.

It is not essential to be a Welsh rugby supporter to sing this hymn,
but it probably helps! The original singers of the hymn, written
250 years ago, were also Welsh, people influenced by the Welsh
revival and wanting to express the joy and excitement of their new
faith in Christ. The famous tune 'Cwm Rhondda' is much more
recent, composed by John Hughes in 1905.

The hymn seems to retain its popularity, even though its
imagery drawn from the book of Exodus in the Old Testament is
increasingly unfamiliar. There are many allusions here to the

Israelites' journey, after their deliverance from Egypt, through the wilderness – 'this barren land' – and across the River Jordan into Canaan, which was to be their new home. It was a long journey, during which they often doubted and disobeyed the Lord. However, he guided them, fed them with manna, 'bread from heaven', quenched their thirst with water from the rock, and reminded them of his presence with them through the signs of fire and cloud. The hymn weaves these experiences of God's people long ago into a prayer that we may experience God now in life and death.

At first it seems to be an entirely 'Old Testament' hymn, with no reference to Jesus Christ. However, 'Bread of heaven' in verse l is in fact Jesus, who referred to himself as 'the bread of life' who 'came down from heaven' (John 6:35, 38. See Chapter 4, page 59). Then, in verse 3, he is also the 'death of deaths and hell's destruction', for by his cross and resurrection he destroyed death and brought people out of their separation from God (which is what hell is) into relationship with God.

Every funeral reminds us of our own mortality, so it is good to sing about 'When I tread the verge of Jordan', when there will be inevitably some 'anxious fear', but hopefully a trust in our complete safety in the Lord.

Hymn: 'Now thank we all our God'

Now thank we all our God,
With heart and hands and voices,
Who wondrous things hath done,
In whom his world rejoices;
Who from our mother's arms
Hath blessed us on our way
With countless gifts of love,
And still is ours today.

O may this bounteous God
Through all our life be near us,
With ever joyful hearts
And blessed peace to cheer us;
And keep us in his grace,
And guide us when perplexed,
And free us from all ills
In this world and the next.

All praise and thanks to God
The Father now be given,
The Son, and him who reigns
With them in highest heaven,
The one eternal God,
Whom earth and heaven adore,
For thus it was, is now,
And shall be evermore.

Every funeral has prayers of thanksgiving; here is a hymn of thanksgiving. It started life as a grace to be sung after meals in the home of its author, Martin Rinkart, a German pastor in the seventeenth century. Now it is known and sung around the world.

It may not be so obviously appropriate for a funeral as some hymns but a number of lines echo our thoughts and feelings:

- the many ways in which we, and the person whose death we mourn, have experienced God's blessing 'on our way';
- our need for 'peace to cheer us' and for guidance 'when perplexed', for example, when we wrestle with bereavement, and with the deep issues of life and death which it brings up;
- confidence in God's protection and provision 'in this world and the next'.

The final verse lifts our minds and hearts to the Lord. Only in looking at him can we find a true perspective when we are caught up in the pain of loss and separation.

Finally, a note of some other suitable hymns and songs.

Easter: 'Jesus lives, thy terrors now, Can, O death, no more appal us'; 'The strife is o'er, the battle done'.

The Cross of Christ: 'Rock of Ages, cleft for me'; 'The old rugged cross'; 'There is a green hill far away'; 'There is a Redeemer'.

What God and Jesus mean to us in life and death: 'God be in my head'; 'Great is thy faithfulness'; 'How sweet the name of Jesus sounds'; 'I am the Bread of Life'; 'Lord of all hopefulness'; 'Love divine, all loves excelling'; 'Peace, perfect peace'.

Heaven: 'Amazing grace'; 'For all the saints'.

CHAPTER 7

❧ Talking to God
The prayers

AFTER THE READING(S) and sermon, followed often
by a hymn, there is a change of gear, a change of tone in the service with the prayers. This is marked by a change of posture, sitting with bowed heads or, better still, kneeling before the Lord
to whom we pray. No longer are we listening to someone reading or speaking to us from the front; now we are all addressing
God and we are encouraged to make the words spoken by one
person the prayers from us all. The 'Amen' is our declaration
that this is our prayer also; it means 'So be it', 'Let it be so', 'Yes,
Lord!'

The Psalms and hymns may in fact have been in the form
of prayers and we may have genuinely used them as such, but this
section of prayers can give us the words, space and silence to bring
our thoughts, longings and memories to God in what can be an
emotional but also liberating time. We may find this part of the
service quite difficult to handle, simply because of the space it creates, and because (in a service at a crematorium or cemetery
chapel) the committal, the 'final farewell', is about to follow. However, it can be a very meaningful time of expressing to God what
we most want to say.

Once again, it is a section where it is entirely right for those
planning the service to make choices or at least suggestions of
prayers they would like used. Most services of the different
denominations have a number of set and alternative prayers, but
there is no reason why other appropriate prayers cannot be select-
ed, or even written specially for the service. Ministers who lead

services regularly draw from other forms of service or collections of prayers.

Thanksgiving

There is thanksgiving both for the message of hope declared to us in the readings and sermon, and for the life of the dead person. Sometimes these themes are combined, as in the new prayer in the *Alternative Service Book* (Section 50). In that, there is thanks to God 'for the life of your son/daughter, N, for the love and mercy he received from you and shared among us'. 'N' indicates the use of the person's name; the prayer is meant to be personalised and to collect up the memories and gratitude of the mourners. It is helpful if the minister at this point in the prayer, or in an introductory sentence, encourages the congregation to make their own specific thanks to God, quietly in their hearts. The minister may also mention specific things about the dead person, for example qualities and characteristics which everyone has acknowledged and appreciated.

The same prayer moves on to say that 'above all we rejoice at your gracious promise . . . that we shall rise again at the coming of Christ'. The sure hope of resurrection which undergirds the service from opening sentence to final committal and blessing is described as the supreme cause of thanks to God: 'Above all'. We can look forward as well as backwards. Another prayer in the *ASB* (Section 56) encourages us to 'remember with thanksgiving those whom we love but see no longer'; how much greater should be the thanksgiving that one day we shall see them again, we shall be reunited in enjoying the fullness of life in God's presence.

Petition

It is entirely natural and right to pray for all who mourn, especially the close family and friends, who can be mentioned by name in the prayer. Some suggested prayers imply that the congregation lift the chief mourners to God: 'Those who mourn'. Others are written in the first person, because everyone at a funeral is affected in some way by the death: 'Grant *us* . . .'

Petitions for those who are greatly affected, perhaps even

crushed by the death, are realistic, both in the sense of asking for
what they most need and also because the requests are based on
what God is like and what he has done in Jesus Christ. For example, a beautiful prayer (Section 55 of the *ASB*) has the sentence:
'Grant us a patient faith in time of darkness, and strengthen our
hearts with the knowledge of your love.' Patience, faith and
strength are certainly things to ask for; but how can you believe
when so much around is dark? How can you be aware of God's
love when facing the trauma of death, perhaps in tragic and distressing circumstances? The opening of the prayer states the heart
of the Christian faith, the guarantee of God's love and the basis
for hope: 'Father in heaven, you gave your Son Jesus Christ to
suffering and to death on the cross and raised him to life in glory.'

Another prayer recalls for us that God is 'the giver of all
comfort', and therefore wants the bereaved, by 'casting all their
care on you', to find that it is so. Here is an echo of Psalm 55:22,
one of the opening sentences, and of 1 Peter 5:7.

A more basic petition in a number of alternative prayers is
that concerning our salvation, our own relationship with God, so
that at our death we shall enjoy what we hope the deceased is entering into. One of these is the final prayer in the modern Church of
England service before the commendation and committal. It is
marked as obligatory, and begins 'Grant us, Lord, the wisdom and
the grace to use aright the time that is left to us here on earth.' In
facing up to our own mortality and to eternal issues, the prayer
expresses the need for us to repent (i.e. to turn away from a life
which displeases God) and to follow Jesus Christ because that is
'the way that leads to the fullness of eternal life'.

This same theme of our future life with God is at the heart
of two other popular prayers. (There is an abundance of choice of
petitionary prayers, and only one or two can be used at this point
in the service; however it is possible to include one near the end
of the service after the committal where it is helpful to have space
for personal reflection.) The first is by John Donne, Dean of St
Paul's Cathedral in the early seventeenth century, and included
in the new draft Methodist service:

Bring us, O Lord God,
at our last awakening
into the house and gate of heaven,
to enter into that gate,
and dwell in that house,
where there shall be
no darkness or dazzling,
but one equal light;
no noise or silence,
but one equal music;
no fears nor hopes,
but one equal possession;
no ends nor beginnings,
but one equal eternity;
in the habitation of your glory and dominion,
world without end. *Amen.*

What a marvellous vision of heaven to stretch our imagination and nurture our faith!

The second appears in several services, including the modern Church of England one. It asks the Lord to 'support us all the day long of this troublous life'. (The Methodist service omits the last four words of this opening sentence; life may be very troubled at the time of a funeral, but it may be unduly pessimistic to describe it as always so.) Then, our request is that, at the end of the day, we shall enjoy 'safe lodging, a holy rest, and peace at the last'. As in Donne's prayer, here are several evocative pictures of the after-life.

Intercession

Occasionally the minister can lead a prayer which goes beyond petitions by the congregation for their own needs (and those of the deceased – see the next section) and is an intercession for others. There may be several other families in the community, known or unknown to us, trying to cope with the pain of bereavement; others who are now facing the fear of dying.

We can pray for them as we sympathise with their need.

So, in the Roman Catholic liturgy, there is an intercession 'that those who bear the cross of pain in mind or body may never feel forsaken by God'. In the modern Church of England service, among the selection of additional prayers, we find: 'Show your mercy to the dying; strengthen them with hope, and fill them with the peace and joy of your presence.'

Incidentally, I am aware that this same appreciation of the needs of the dying and bereaved, which can be expressed at the service in such intercession, may later lead several people into becoming bereavement visitors or counsellors. Their experience can benefit others.

Commendation

This is the prayer in which we entrust the dead person to God by name. It is an expression of our faith in 'the mercy of God our Maker and Redeemer' (*ASB* service) and in his desire and ability to keep him safe. We do not have to 'recommend' him to God or remind him of their good qualities (see the comments in Chapter 5 on not making the sermon a eulogy). God does not require a reference before he takes them on! The good news is always that the basis of eternal life is in God's love and forgiveness, not in our achievements.

Beyond the simple commending and entrusting of the deceased to the Lord, there is a considerable division of opinion in the Christian Church as to whether it is right to pray for the dead. For some, it is entirely natural to continue to pray for those who we prayed for when they were alive. For others, it seems unnecessary if they are now entirely safe with Christ beyond death. So you will find that the Catholic service includes such petitions, the Free Church orders avoid them, and the modern Church of England service has some which carefully reflect the agreement (or compromise?) suggested by a Doctrine Commission report, 'Prayer and the Departed' (SPCK, 1971). The Anglican prayers exclude any thoughts of asking God to give what he has not already promised and guaranteed; they are further expressions of entrusting the deceased to God or looking forward to the whole Church in glory. So, in the prayer after the commendation, the wording is: 'Bring the whole church, living and departed in the Lord Jesus, to a joyful resurrection . . .' There is also no hint that we have some kind of second chance after death to decide to believe in God. Prayers for the dead have to reflect the difficult fact that people make irrevocable choices for or against God in this life, but also the exciting fact that God's promise of eternal life is also irrevocable to all who believe in him.

The Lord's Prayer

Most services provide for the use of this, the Christian family prayer, at some point. Nowadays, the problem is the variety of versions – traditional, modified and modern. So in saying the prayer together it is very helpful to be able to follow the words in the service book or on a specially printed service sheet. To use this familiar prayer creates one of the valuable ways in which the congregation can be actively involved, not just listening or watching.

This book is not the place for a detailed look at this prayer which Jesus taught his followers, but we should notice the petition for forgiveness, 'Forgive us our trespasses as we forgive those who trespass against us'. There can be strong feelings of guilt and anger around, especially as the bereaved blame themselves or others for what has happened or for the lack of care and support of the loved one in the period before their death. Sometimes there is real guilt, things to feel ashamed of, things to regret, perhaps which have characterised the relationship over many years. More often, the guilt is vastly exaggerated out of all proportion. There is always more that could have been done, but frequently those who think this have in fact been caring sacrificially anyway. Any faults in the caring and loving cannot now be made up for; therefore they seem unrealistically serious.

At funerals, apart from some who sense a need for forgiveness, there may be those in the circle of family and friends who need to forgive each other. The gathering together at the funeral can quickly bring to the fore tensions and recriminations which have never been dealt with. For example, grown-up children of the deceased may have grown apart from each other or from their parents, or the deceased or their widow/widower may have been married (or had partners) more than once, and there is no love lost between the different branches of the family.

With so many different emotions around at a funeral, it is not an easy time to talk through the issues, but the very sharing together in the grief can be a trigger for some new starts. The clause in the Lord's Prayer can become particularly meaningful in such circumstances.

CHAPTER 8

❧ Goodbye and farewell
The committal

WHEN THE WHOLE SERVICE is held at the crematorium chapel, the committal follows on immediately after the prayer of commendation. When the main service has been in church or a cemetery chapel, there is a journey (of many miles or a few yards) to the graveside or the crematorium for committal. If the journey is lengthy, not all the mourners may travel to the committal, but it is a part of the funeral which the family are often most apprehensive about and when they need the support of others.

The committal seems to be the final farewell to the loved one. This can be so, even for those who were present at the time of death or have subsequently seen the body in the home, hospital or chapel of rest. It can be like a farewell, even for those who appreciate the very important distinction between the commendation of the dead person by name into the hands of God and the committal of their body, which they no longer need, to cremation or the grave (or occasionally, the sea).

For some people, the shock and grief of bereavement is accompanied by almost a disbelief that the loved one really has died, has gone. In addition, several bereaved people have the sensation, which can continue long after the funeral, that 'they are still with me', particularly in the familiar places where much time had been spent together. So the committal, often a very short ceremony, is more than a functional task of disposing of the body. It helps the family and friends to face the reality of the death, to acknowledge the separation which has taken place, and to believe that the Christian hope includes the idea of a resurrection body –

which will enable us to meet and recognise each other again.

The committal can mark the separation and express our farewells because, even if we truly believe the person has gone into the safe keeping of the Lord, their body was so much part of that person we knew and loved. Furthermore, the physical presence of the body at the service enables the separation and farewell to be marked in symbolic ways, for example touching the coffin, sprinkling with holy water and incensing of the body (see Chapter 9), lowering it into the grave, or the closing of curtains at the crematorium.

In the Catholic rite, there can be a Song of Farewell at the committal. The new Methodist service, immediately after the committal, suggests the use of a traditional Christian farewell: 'Go forth upon your journey from this world, O Christian soul . . .' This same farewell or commendation is suggested for use in the Church of England in prayers with a dying person or at the time of death, where it may seem to be more strictly appropriate, but there is no denying the impact of such words (and the symbolic actions mentioned earlier) at this point in the funeral.

There is also important symbolism in what happens, particularly at a crematorium, when the words of committal are spoken. The practical layout of chapels varies but usually the coffin is lowered, or rolls back through doors, as some curtains close in front of the coffin. The physical movement (and also the mechanical noises) can be very distressing, because it does symbolise separation and farewell. (It is debatable whether music at this stage helps – it can sound sentimental, even Hollywood-esque.) Therefore, some people request that the coffin remain in place, left in view even when the mourners leave. It is worth saying that although, for some, this is the way to manage almost intolerable grief and emotion, the symbolism of the body being taken from them is very important in enabling them to face the fact of death and let the person go. These are painful but necessary steps in the bereavement process. The movement of the coffin (or curtains) at the crematorium and the lowering of the coffin at the grave (and the covering with earth by members of the family as for example in some Afro-Caribbean funerals) are symbols of the fact that indeed the person has been taken from us. They really have gone from us. To leave behind the body in the chapel with the coffin still visible can be a way of denying this reality.

Of course the committal, with its sharp focusing on the fact of death, is set within the context of the positive message of the funeral as a whole. Where it takes place before or after a service in church, there is provision for the extra reading of Scripture verses and for prayers to help the mourners hold on to God and trust in his provision of eternal life for his people. So, in the modern Church of England service, possible readings include Revelation 14:13: 'I heard a voice from heaven saying, "Write this: 'Happy are the dead who die in the faith of Christ . . .'"' and some verses from Psalm 103 (see Chapter 3, page 42). The rather sobering words of the ancient anthem can be used here which begins 'Man born of a woman has but a short time to live' but end with the confident prayer 'Forgive us our sins and at our last hour let us not fall away from you'. After the committal, Psalm 16:11 is read: 'God will show us the path of life . . .' Other services have similar readings before and after.

The *words of committal* emphasise the future hope: 'In sure and certain hope of the resurrection to eternal life through Jesus Christ our Lord'. The Christian faith takes the body very seriously. Our physical bodies on earth are part of God's creation and their committal and disposal at the end is done with dignity and respect. In a sense it is the final act of caring for the person (body and soul) who has died. In the life to come, Christians believe there will be a resurrection of the body, not just the immortality of the soul. To be sure, it will be a body without the limitations and frailty of physical existence on earth. But it will be recognisably the same person. This belief is based on the gospel accounts of Jesus after his resurrection. After a period of shock and disbelief, the disciples realised that Jesus was with them, albeit with a body now fitted for eternal life with God. In his great chapter on resurrection (1 Corinthians 15) St Paul states that we shall know the same transformation: 'just as we have borne the likeness of the earthly man, so shall we bear the likeness of the man from heaven' (v. 49). The traditional Church of England service, in the words of committal, quotes some similar teaching from Paul in his letter to the Philippians: 'who shall change the body of our low estate that it may be like unto his glorious body'.

The new resurrection body is not built from the remains of the old but is a new creation by God. There need be no anxiety about this for the relatives as they decide whether there should be cremation or burial, or in circumstances where the funeral has to take place without the body. This can be the result of an accident or a miscarriage (see Chapter 10), or where the body has been left to medical research (in which case there may be a committal at a later stage).

After the words of committal, there is usually provision for at least a prayer and blessing. The modern Church of England service feels unnecessarily brief and abrupt at this point with just the reading of Psalm 16:11 and an ascription of praise to God: 'Unto him that is able to keep us from falling . . .' There needs to be time to be quiet, to pray and to be prayed for. The music, as the congregation leaves the crematorium chapel, can also help to create the right atmosphere of hope and victory.

 POSTSCRIPT
Resurrection or reincarnation?

Increasingly we live in a society where people feel free to pick and choose, from various traditions and faiths, the religious ideas and experiences which they find most attractive. Reincarnation is apparently considered by some church members and by several others with a basically Christian viewpoint to be a convincing concept which can be 'bolted on' to their other beliefs. It is part of the attractiveness of Eastern religions, including Hinduism, for those who are puzzled by Christianity, worried by its disputes, or just interested in possible alternatives. Of course these alternatives are now believed and lived out by large faith communities within our own country.

My aim in this Postscript is not to analyse or express my doubts about reincarnation in any great detail, but rather to point out that it is not, and cannot logically be, part of the Christian faith.

The Christian funeral service recognises the uniqueness of each human life and, by commending the person into God's loving care, clearly looks forward to a resurrection life beyond this world. Christians base these beliefs on the teaching of Jesus and on his death and resurrection; he was the pioneer of the way we shall take.

One of the attractive features of reincarnation must be the idea that, given enough opportunities (even hundreds or thousands of lives), we shall get it right and be worthy of heaven. However, my knowledge of myself and other people only underlines the Christian view that no one's life is perfect or deserving of heaven; all of us are always dependent on the infinite love and mercy of God. So, reincarnation may remove the idea of judgment, but to my mind includes the unrealistic expectation that we shall get our lives perfectly right in the end, or build up sufficient merit.

Another aspect of reincarnation which I find unconvincing is the sense of living a whole series of reincarnations, but not being aware or having any recollection of previous existences. (I know there are examples of people who claim to recall details of a former life; I do not pretend to understand this, but I know they are very rare.) In what sense am I the same as in my earlier lives, if there is no memory? I find the idea of continuity of 'soul', but not of my personality, very unsatisfying. For example, for me, one of the joys of heaven will be reunion, picking up relationships, remembering experiences we have shared. I suppose the Hindu idea of our personalities being absorbed into God at the end, rather than having unique and fulfilling relationships with him, means that the lack of conscious continuity between our series of lives on earth or between earth and heaven matters less.

So much more could be said on this vast and complicated subject, but my aim here is to point out how reincarnation does not fit in with the Christian beliefs about our salvation through the love of God in Christ, not through our own merits or perfection, and about our relationship with God in the glory of heaven. The Christian funeral proclaims, not the prospect of further reincarnations, but the hope of resurrection into the new world God has prepared for us.

CHAPTER 9

🎵 More than words can say
Signs, symbols and rituals

THE FUNERAL SERVICE can feel full of words – and words which, for those not very familiar with Christian worship and teaching, seem at times technical or strange. This is not to deny the importance of the words. The Christian Gospel is good news, something to proclaim, a message of life and hope, which people need to hear and respond to. The words of the Bible itself, in the Psalms and other readings, and often reflected in the language of hymns and prayers, have a special authority and significance for the Christian.

However, the impact of the service comes from more than the meaning of the words. For example, the way in which the service is led and the words are spoken will convey so much – for good or ill. Wonderful words spoken by a minister who does not seem to care about the congregation or to believe deeply in what he is saying quickly lose their significance and power. On the other hand, people often make a comment after a funeral something like: 'Although I can't remember all he said, I was struck by the fact that he really seemed to believe it.' There is also the impact on the bereaved of being surrounded by family and friends, some of whom may have travelled long distances to be there. The words of sympathy – on the day, and in letters, cards and telephone calls – mean a lot, but their readiness to come to the service speaks volumes in terms of respect for the deceased and support for the bereaved.

In an earlier chapter we considered the words of some of the great hymns which can be chosen for a funeral, but there is also the power of the music itself whether it is to be sung or not. Organ or other instrumental music at the start and ending of the funeral can help to create the right atmosphere and to underline the meaning of the service. One of the notes in the Catholic 'Order of Christian Funerals' puts it like this: 'Well-chosen music can touch the mourners and others present at levels of human need that words alone often fail to reach.'

Then there are the more specifically Christian symbols and signs used within the service. They are more likely to be encountered in Catholic funerals but are increasingly adopted, at least as options, in other churches too. If you have attended funerals you may have been impressed or puzzled by some of them. If you are involved in planning a service, you may want to suggest the adoption of some of them, although this may need to be dependent on the tradition of the local church or of the minister leading the service. Generally it is true that what we do or see is at least as powerful as what we say or hear in strengthening our faith and pointing us to God. The proviso of course is that any symbolism must reinforce the heart of the Christian faith rather than obscure it.

The Eucharist, or Holy Communion, is the most powerful proclamation of Christ's death and resurrection. However, it is rarely part of the funeral service outside the 'Funeral Mass' of the Roman Catholic Church and of the 'high church' tradition within the Church of England. Even then, it is usually only used if the deceased and/or the family were members of the church. Here is a service which focuses our attention clearly on the Christian hope. There is praise to God for Christ's victory over sin and death, praise which is offered 'with angels and archangels and with the whole company of heaven'. The service is a foretaste of the 'heavenly banquet', that biblical picture for heaven as a place of life, sharing and celebration. In sharing bread and wine, the worshippers are reminded of the eternal life which Christ has won for them and given to them. It is a service which provides a very obvious context in which prayers can be offered, commending the deceased to God's love and mercy.

The other great Christian sacrament – baptism – is sometimes recalled in the funeral service by the use of holy water and a white pall (a white cloth which is placed over the coffin). In the Roman Catholic liturgy the sprinkling of the coffin with holy water at the door of the church and at the commendation is a reminder of the water of baptism which marks the start of the Christian life. It is through this washing and cleansing by God that people are brought into an eternal relationship with him. The funeral is another step in that living relationship. What God promised at baptism still holds good.

The white pall is now an option in the Methodist service as well as a traditional part of the Catholic funeral. It recalls the white garments perhaps worn at baptism, but more than that it symbolises the putting on of new life, the putting on of Christ. Baptism speaks of a washing away of sin and also of being clothed in Christ, i.e. a new start, in which God looks not on the mess of our lives but on the goodness of Jesus Christ to whom we belong. At death the Christian goes to meet God, still relying on Christ, instead of on his own record of achievement in life; the white pall can be a powerful symbol of this basis of hope.

Another strong symbol is the Paschal Candle, so called because it is first lit at the Easter celebrations. It represents the presence of the resurrected and living Christ among his people – the source of our comfort and strength and the guarantee of our sharing in his victory over death.

It is possible to choose or encounter the use of several other signs and symbols, for example incense, a Bible or cross on the coffin, candles around the coffin, and photographs, mementoes and tools of the person's work. The danger here is obviously having such a variety that the power and simplicity of the symbolism is lost or confused.

Earlier in the chapter we mentioned the impact of being surrounded by friends and family at such a time. Increasingly there is encouragement for them (and, indeed, for the chief mourners) to take some active part in the funeral, if they feel able. This could include reading the lesson or some prayers, as well as spreading the pall over the coffin, bringing up the bread and wine for the Eucharist, carrying the Bible or cross to place on the coffin. It is traditional in, for example, Afro-Caribbean funerals, for the men to carry the coffin and to fill in the grave. Participating like this in the service can express a support for and an identification with the other mourners and a respect for the deceased; it can also be a way of expressing and working through one's own grief. As with making decisions about the planning and preparation of a funeral service, this involvement seems increasingly significant in an age when so many of us are distanced from the process and fact of death, and when many of the old rituals of mourning, such as closing the curtains, preparing the body, wearing black, have gone.

 ## POSTSCRIPT
'What should I wear?' 'Where do I sit?'
'What about flowers?'

Clothes

It is almost impossible to generalise. Certainly people wear a much wider range of clothes to ordinary church services nowadays, and this trend spills over to funerals. However, most funerals are dignified occasions with elements of formality, and this may guide your choice of what to wear. This does not necessarily mean everyone should wear something black or dark as a mark of respect to the deceased and the family. Trust your intuition and your knowledge of the family.

I have known families which have made special requests for mourners not to wear dark clothing, because they wanted the service to be primarily a celebration of the life which had ended and of the Christian hope. I still vividly remember the funeral service twenty-five years ago of the daughter of some close personal friends. She died at the age of 15 after a year's painful struggle with cancer. For the service, her mother bought a bright new outfit – red and navy blue. She said to me she would have chosen something similar if her daughter had been getting married, so it

also seemed appropriate for this occasion as she went to be with
Jesus Christ and enjoy fullness of life in glory. Everyone at the
service knew that this was no denial of the death, or of the deep
grief and sorrow. It was however a wonderful visual proclamation
of the Christian hope.

Seating

At most services in a crematorium chapel everyone enters
together, immediately before or after the coffin, and therefore is
guided into seats, filling up from the front. However if, as a member of the congregation, you are claustrophobic or feel panicky
near the front, it's all right to slip into a seat where you feel easier. Sometimes at the crematorium, the rest of the mourners will
be taken in before the immediate family, and in this case the necessary number of chairs or pews will be left free at the front of the
chapel on one or both sides of the aisle.

Similarly, for a church service, those arranging the service
will need to tell the funeral directors how many seats to reserve
for close family and friends. As the rest of the congregation enter
the church beforehand, they are free to sit anywhere although
often the minister, verger or funeral director is on hand to guide
those who are unsure. Regularly I notice that people leave not only
the required rows free, but also several immediately behind those,
so that when the immediate family enter, they are sitting in splen-
did, or rather embarrassing, isolation. It's good to have people just
behind them; they may feel awkward and conspicuous anyway,
and if they are not able to sing much, at least others near them will
make up for their lack!

Flowers and donations

The sending of flowers is a wonderful way of expressing
sympathy. Obviously they can add beauty to the service itself, but
suitable flowers can also be a delight to the bereaved in their home
before and after the funeral. Funeral directors will usually have
ideas of where some flowers could be sent after the service (e.g.
hospital or residential homes). Several bereaved families these

days give friends a choice of sending flowers or making a donation to some charity. Usually only a few of the flowers are actually on view in the service, and people may feel that the money would be better used through helping others. The wishes of the family will be known through the wording of the newspaper notice, or by simply asking the funeral director or a family member. It can save embarrassment if wishes about flowers are respected, particularly if it is 'Family flowers only'. You must feel free about whether, or how much, to donate to any charity mentioned. In addition, remember a brief card or letter can convey your thoughts and love, even if the sending of flowers is not appropriate.

CHAPTER 10

❧ Let the children come to me

Funerals of children

The funeral service for a child

With the death of a child, a wonderful gift so recently given seems to have been snatched away. It is right that the service should proclaim God's love and the Christian hope of eternal life, but there can be no neat explanations or answers for why death has come so soon. In the intense grief and emptiness and perplexity of the parents and of other close family and friends, the question may be asked – perhaps with understandable anger or despair – but there are no clever solutions. We do not know why we live in a world of illness, accidents and severe disabilities. They seem to come arbitrarily into people's lives. Christians do not believe God singles people out in some revengeful or judgmental way. But why, in a world God has made, are there such risks, such horrifying events? We do not really know.

The Bible speaks of a world which is spoilt, has gone wrong, but which one day will be perfectly re-made and restored. However, at the very time when deep questions may be asked, the funeral service for a child gives no further clues. What the service does proclaim strongly is the love and care of a God who does not stand aloof from the human situation but came to earth and was involved in it. In the gospels we read about Jesus facing pain, bereavement and death. We also see a particular concern for children, their dignity and worth, which was in sharp contrast to the attitudes of many people of his day.

The Christian funeral service also speaks positively of the hope of life with God for the child who has died. This can be done with even greater assurance than at the funeral of an adult, because many Christians believe that it is possible for adults to reject God's love and to opt out of a relationship with him (see the Postscript to Chapter 2). However, a child is completely safe with God. What Jesus Christ has done by his death and resurrection to bring the world back to God and to belong to him for ever most certainly applies to children. They are covered by God's plan and purpose of love for his people, even if they never had a chance to hear, understand or personally respond to it.

In this context, it may be helpful to comment on the standing of children who die unbaptised. Hardly any Christian today would believe that the absence of baptism affects the child's relationship with their heavenly Father. In the Catholic 'Order of Christian Funerals' there are some alternative prayers (of commendation, etc.) to be said when the child died before baptism, but these do not express any less confidence in God's embracing love for the child. What is omitted is any reference to the particular meaning and symbolism of baptism. This expression of confidence in the position of the unbaptised child is not to deny the powerful reassurance of an 'emergency baptism' which parents may request after the birth of a very sick baby or when a child is suddenly taken ill.

So, the funeral of a child boldly speaks of the future. At a time when there may be few memories, only the realisation of a life cut short, so much potential unrealised, there is the hope of fullness of life. In the New Testament we are not given many details of what the resurrection life will be like. Yet it is reasonable to suggest that it will be the fulfilment of all our potential, the expression of all that we are. Therefore the person we knew for example as a new-born baby or as someone with severe physical or mental disabilities will, in the life to come, live and be recognised in their full humanity.

There is a phrase in some of the services of the different denominations about the God who has made nothing in vain. A life cut short seems to us a desperate waste, but it is not so in the context of eternity.

In recent years, most denominations have made more specific provision for the funerals of children. For example, the Church of England in its modern *Alternative Service Book* has a separate service, and most of the comments which follow will relate to material in that service, although with some references to what other churches use. (In the book used at most crematoria, the service is not printed separately, but there are indications of material which is relevant to a child's funeral.)

The opening sentence
The following is to be used, but other sentences of Scripture (see Chapter 2) may also be added.

The Lamb who is at the centre of the throne will be their shepherd; he will lead them to springs of living water. And God will wipe away every tear from their eyes.
(Revelation 7:17)

The last book of the Bible, with its often perplexing imagery and symbolism, has some vivid and powerful descriptions of heaven which were intended to encourage those first-century Christians facing hardship and persecution. Their reassurance was in the fact that God would have the last word; the victory was his over evil and death and all that spoils this life. The reality of heaven was emphasised. The verse above is at the end of a section about 'a great multitude that no-one could count, from every nation, tribe, people and language, standing before the throne' (v. 9). (It is sometimes read as a lesson at a funeral service.)

The opening sentence for the service has some clear echoes of Psalm 23, 'The Lord is my shepherd' – which is the set Psalm for a child's funeral. It also links up with Jesus' words in John's gospel: 'I am the good shepherd'. Why is this verse chosen to start the service? The picture of God as shepherd can apply to people of any age but there is the fact that sheep, and especially lambs, are completely dependent on the shepherd for refreshment, protection and guidance, as are babies and young children on adults and on God himself. In a sense, the parents can safely pass on the responsibility for their child to the Lord.

Interestingly, Jesus Christ is referred to in the verse both as shepherd and as lamb. 'The Lamb' is a common title for him in the book of Revelation. At the start of his ministry, Jesus was described as 'the lamb of God' by John the Baptist. The description is based on the Jewish sacrificial system and sees Jesus' death on the cross in terms of sacrifice deliberately made for the forgiveness and the life of others. The New Testament writers particularly linked the crucifixion with a famous passage in Isaiah, chapter 53, which includes these phrases about a suffering servant of God: 'Surely he took up our infirmities and carried our sorrows' and 'He was led like a lamb to the slaughter'.

It is in the realisation that Jesus was a lamb in this sense himself which gives Christians the reassurance (even the guarantee) that he can be trusted to act as the loving shepherd of his own sheep and lambs. His commitment to us is not in doubt.

'And God will wipe away every tear.' Hopefully adults are not immune to tears as an expression of, and outlet for, their feelings particularly at a funeral. But we especially associate tears with babies and young children, and it is the wise parent who knows instinctively what they mean – messages often without words. God perfectly interprets and understands the needs and longings of each individual, including children. Again there is the sense that he can be trusted with our children who have gone to him.

The Church of England service set out in the traditional *Book of Common Prayer* suggests a similar sentence from the book of Isaiah in the Old Testament: 'He shall feed his flock like a shepherd; he shall gather the lambs with his arms, and carry them in his bosom' (Isaiah 40:11).

The Readings
Either or both of Mark 10:13–16, and Ephesians 3:14–19 are set. The Mark passage is more commonly used, and is also suggested by other churches' forms of service.

People were bringing little children to Jesus to have him touch them, but the disciples rebuked them. When Jesus saw this, he was indignant. He said to them, 'Let the little children come to me, and do not hinder them, for the kingdom of God belongs to such as these. I tell you the truth, anyone who will not receive the kingdom of God like a little child will never enter it.' And he took the children in his arms, put his hands on them and blessed them.

(Mark 10:13–16)

Jesus had time for children. His disciples assumed he would not want to be troubled, as if he had more important people to meet. Jesus was annoyed by that attitude; he gave children time, honour and dignity. God's kingdom includes children and others like them, i.e. those who are prepared to receive what God has for them. So, the action and words of Jesus are the prime source of our confidence that children are safe with God for eternity and can be commended to him in faith and assurance.

Some *prayers of commendation* refer directly or indirectly to Jesus' taking children in his arms. The Methodist and Roman Catholic services ask God to take/receive the child into his arms or into his 'embrace' or 'the arms of his mercy'. It is very comforting and encouraging language.

The age of the children in Mark 10 is not clear. They were brought, not necessarily carried, but at the end Jesus 'took the children in his arms' – although some translations have 'put his arms around them'. Perhaps it is good that we cannot be specific; the incident may have included young babies and also children of infant and junior ages, and can be validly applied to that age range today.

The funeral service for a stillborn or newly born child, and following a miscarriage

Most Christian churches are now prepared to offer a funeral service in these tragic circumstances, and indeed some have recently offered a form of service which can be used. For example, the Church of England has a section of 'Prayers after the birth of a stillborn child or the death of a newly born child' which can be used in church, hospital or home, and 'where appropriate they may be used at the burial or cremation'. In the Catholic 'Order of Christian Funerals', there is a 'Rite of Final Commendation for an Infant' which may be used in the case of a stillborn or newly born infant, 'or may be adapted for use with parents who have suffered a miscarriage'. Obviously, given the Roman Catholic Church's strong opposition to abortion, it is unlikely that the Rite would ever be used at such a time, but other churches would probably respond to a request from a parent who realises that, because of extreme medical or other circumstances, a life has been lost.

Stillbirths and the deaths of babies are so much rarer than they used to be, but of course that means they are even more unexpected and traumatic. Such an occurrence is a real bereavement, and a funeral service helps the parents to grieve, and to mark the fact of a life as well as a death. (In the case of a stillborn child, both the birth and the death have to be registered.) Parents can authorise the hospital to arrange the funeral of a baby who has been stillborn or died within a few hours of birth (and they can still attend if they wish), but increasingly parents make funeral arrangements with a funeral director. It may be important for the parents to give the child a name, if they have not already chosen one, and for this name to be used in the service as an acknowledgment of the unique life, the unique person, who has died.

This has been a sadly neglected area in the offering of help to the bereaved, but now the churches and bereavement counsellors (and excellent agencies such as the Stillbirth and Neonatal Death Society – address in Appendix C) are helping parents to deal with a real loss.

Many Christians would believe that a miscarriage is also an event where a life (not just a potential life) has been lost, and where feelings of bereavement are entirely natural and not to be played down by glib phrases like 'I am sure you'll soon be pregnant again.' There may in fact be fears about future pregnancies and about what the parents did which might have 'caused' the miscarriage, as well as a deep sense of loss and grieving.

Here then are circumstances where a funeral service can be requested, and the order of service chosen with the same care and involvement as for the death of someone older. The service should be personalised; strangely the Church of England prayers do not assume the child's name will be used. In the Catholic Rite, there is provision for parents who have suffered a miscarriage to name the child, if they so wish – 'We now wish to name this little one N., a name we shall treasure in our hearts for ever.'

As with a funeral for an older child, the service for a still-born or newborn baby contains confident words of commendation of the child to God's merciful keeping, and prayers which seek God's comfort for parents and family in their genuine distress and sorrow. Also, one of the Church of England prayers affirms of God: 'You make nothing in vain, and love all that you have made.' The life, however short-lived on earth (or even just in the womb) has a uniqueness and a destiny in God's loving purpose. One day there will be reunion, and we shall appreciate the full potential of the life God made.

The presence of children and young people at funerals

Far fewer children and young people seem to attend funerals these days than in the past. The exception is when it is a friend from school or college who has died. Otherwise, it seems that they are discouraged from coming or parents simply assume they will not attend and perhaps make other provision for them during the time of the service.

It may be right to question this increasing trend. Of course there are several factors in this, including the longer life expectancy in our society and the breakdown of family ties, so that comparatively few children face the death of a parent, and they may have slender links with the grandfather or great aunt who has died. However, we live in a society in which people are increasingly distanced from the fact and reality of death. For example, most die in hospital rather than at home, the dead body is rarely seen, and there is less use of the rituals and customs which marked a death in the family. We are now in danger of passing on to the next generation this avoidance or denial of death, and therefore leaving it ill-equipped to know how to cope with loss and bereavement at different stages in their lives.

It is dangerous to be dogmatic as to whether children should attend a funeral. 'It depends on who has died, the age of the child, the attitudes of the family, and the form of service to be used' (*Letting Go* – Ian Ainsworth Smith and Peter Speck; New Library of Pastoral Care, SPCK, 1982).

Probably more children should be given the option of attending. This means that parents and others would need to explain about the death, and about the details of the service. Sometimes, young children can be more matter-of-fact about death, and also gain from being treated as part of a family in mourning and sorrow.

The Roman Catholic services encourage children or young people to be involved where possible in the funeral of a brother or sister, of a classmate or friend; for example in music, readings or prayers. Once again, in the planning of a service, it is important to be aware of these options and possibilities. Particularly in this question of children and young people attending and even participating, adults should not be over-protective or project on to them their own fear of not being able to cope in the service.

CHAPTER 11

❧ The longer journey
Services and prayers before and after the funeral itself

IN SITUATIONS WHERE the dead person or the close family have been regular churchgoers, some of the services and ceremonies listed in this chapter will often be regarded as 'extras', which they want and expect. This is particularly true for members of the Roman Catholic Church which, in its 'Order of Christian Funerals', makes rich and varied provision for the time between the death itself and the funeral service. Other churches are beginning to produce possible services for this period.

It is important to realise with this, as with other aspects of the planning and preparations following the death, that you can ask for and opt in to some of the opportunities, usually brief, to focus on God and receive from the ministry of the church. If you have not been churchgoers, the funeral director and even the minister may assume you would not want them. But you only have to ask!

Prayers in the home

If the minister is present at the moment of death or soon afterwards, he can lead a very simple service, with a few verses from a Psalm or a gospel, and some prayers, usually including the Lord's Prayer. It will probably last three or four minutes. The same service can be used at the bedside in hospital, or at a later stage when the minister meets the family at home to begin to plan the funeral. The family can always say it does not seem appropriate or they do not feel able to cope, but usually the prayers and reading can calm their emotions and point them towards the Christian hope.

The Church of England now has a service (to be considered in the next section) which is primarily used if the body is brought to church the day before the funeral, but 'alternatively, this service may be said in the home before the body is taken to church'. The Roman Catholics have a similar ceremony entitled 'Gathering of the family and transfer of the body to the church or to the place of committal'. These days the family and close friends may meet together for the first time since the death only on the funeral day itself. Indeed it is increasingly common not to accompany the body from the house, but to meet the hearse and also other friends and family at the church or chapel. Whatever the circumstances, there is the possibility of prayer in the home on the day, before setting out for the funeral service.

'A Service which may be used before the Funeral'

I referred above to this service, set out in the Church of England's *Alternative Service Book*. It has similarities to the Roman Catholic form of reception of the body at the church and also to its service of 'Vigil for the deceased'. The Methodist Church now also has suggested material for a Vigil.

Such a service would usually take place during the late afternoon or evening before the funeral. The outline of the Church of England service is very simple:

A sentence of Scripture.
The reading – Romans 8:31–9 (see my comment on page 61).
Verses from Psalms 27 and 139.
Prayers, including the Lord's Prayer.

The service can serve a number of purposes. It may be a small and private occasion, perhaps when a death has occurred in very distressing circumstances; and it can be the opportunity for the family to adjust to seeing the coffin in its place for the funeral. It may be a time when several friends and members of the local community, who might not be able to attend the funeral service, can come to support the mourners. It may be regarded as the practical preparation for the body to be in church overnight, with all the reassuring symbolism of being in the Lord's house.

The burial of ashes

The majority of funerals in this country now involve cremation rather than burial. This means there is a further decision about what should be done with the ashes. Families can be taken by surprise when the question is raised by the funeral director or minister; sometimes the result is a snap decision which they may have some regrets about later. Those leaving instructions for their own funerals can helpfully express preferences for the place of burial of ashes after cremation; for example, burial in an existing family grave may not otherwise be considered by the relatives as a possibility.

The burial of ashes completes the task of reverently disposing of the body of the loved one. With cremation this is inevitably a two-stage process. In the funeral service there is the committal of the body 'to be cremated'; in the Church of England's very brief service 'at the internment of the ashes' there is a further committal 'to the ground'. The words 'earth to earth, ashes to ashes, dust to dust' are sometimes added. Even where no religious ceremony is to take place (as in the majority of cases), a decision has to be made about this second stage.

Many people ask for the ashes to be disposed of by the crematorium, which usually has a Garden of Remembrance where they can be buried. Sometimes this is done to avoid the problem of further arrangements or the pain and emotion of another ceremony. Often it is the natural decision, because there is no obvious alternative – or at least the relatives are not aware of one. To choose dispersal of ashes at the crematorium does not leave you without a place of remembering, even if there is no grave to tend. There is the Garden itself, and often the option of placing a small plaque in the area, or paying for a plant (usually a rose) for the garden.

Many churchyards and some cemeteries now have a special area set aside for burying ashes, and the minister can lead the brief ceremony if the family wish it. This is usually within a few days of the funeral but can be later, even much later, if that is when the close family are next able to meet together. Often however the ceremony is performed with one or two closest mourners.

It can be appropriate to bury ashes in an existing family grave, even where there is no room for another coffin. Some additional inscription on the memorial stone, or a small plaque, is usually allowed. Such plaques are not always possible in the new Gardens of Remembrance in churchyards, but even so for many people they become places of revisiting and remembering, where flowers can be left and where a Book of Remembrance is usually housed nearby, open at the relevant anniversary day or month.

Some who are bereaved find it very important emotionally to have a place of remembering. This is just as possible when cremation is followed by burial of ashes as when there is the burial of the coffin, although in many Gardens of Remembrance the exact spot of burial may not be marked. Other people do not regard such a place as crucial in their process of coping with their bereavement. Anyway, it may not be a real possibility if the family live at a considerable distance from where the deceased lived and died. A place of burial, even if marked and commemorated, may rarely be visited – but just an annual visit can of course have great significance to some.

The burial of ashes, as with the committal at a burial or cremation, is a forward-looking ceremony: 'in sure and certain hope of the resurrection to eternal life through our Lord Jesus Christ, who died, was buried, and rose again for us'. Even when the burial of ashes in the crematorium Garden is without a service and therefore the repeat of these words, it can be regarded as an extension of the committal already spoken. However, I need to refer to the number of special requests where ashes are taken away by the relatives and disposed of in unusual or bizarre ways – scattered on a football pitch or bowling green, an area of beautiful countryside, at sea, etc. While an important aspect of the funeral is remembering the life and interests, the work and hobbies of the deceased, disposal of ashes in these ways runs counter to the Christian desire to look forward to the person's future existence with God. We need to turn our focus from this world to the world of God's new creation.

Times to remember

'I shall feel relieved in a few days' time when the funeral is over.' It can be seen as a hurdle, a daunting occasion, with calmer days beyond. Yet the planning and preparation for a funeral gives the bereaved something to do and focus upon, when their world is upside down and life has lost direction. It is also a time when family, friends and neighbours gather to console and help practically.

After the funeral, with family scattered again and a return to 'routine', the pain of loss and loneliness can at times be very acute. Even after many months, the strong feelings can sweep over again, just when it was thought things were settling down. It is important therefore that, in addition to any network of friends and family, the churches and other organisations can offer the help of 'visitors' or sometimes 'counsellors' to give the bereaved a chance to talk privately and express what they are feeling.

Many churches also arrange public occasions for remembering; occasions which, like the funeral itself, can express thanksgiving, sorrow and hope. In a few areas of the country, families still attend the local church on the Sunday after the funeral. Certainly churches would be offering prayers for such families around the time of the funeral. Prayers are also offered in a number of churches on the Sunday nearest to the anniversary of the death, sometimes called 'the year's mind'. Some churches, which have a large number of funerals, hold monthly requiem or memorial services, and invite relatives who have been bereaved during the month. (It is of course permitted to attend more than one!) Many more churches have an annual service, usually at the start of November (2nd November is All Souls Day). Apart from hymns, readings and prayers (and perhaps Holy Communion), the names of the dead are read out and occasionally there is a ceremony in which relatives can light a candle as an expression of thanksgiving and prayer to God.

CHAPTER 12

And finally . . .

ONE OF THE AIMS of this book has been to encourage personal and informed choices and decisions about one's own funeral or that of a close relative and friend. So I want to finish with a hymn I have chosen for my own funeral: a hymn mainly written by Charles Wesley, the great eighteenth-century Methodist hymnwriter, but with a few additions by others.

My attention was first drawn to it by reading the biography of Dr William Sangster, the Methodist minister who was at the Central Hall, Westminster for sixteen years, including the whole of the Second World War, and died in 1960. I never met him or even heard him preach, but he was a kind of hero-figure for me with his London roots, his passion for the sharing of the Christian Gospel, and his marvellous preaching.

Wesley's great funeral hymn, which Sangster called 'the only supremely great hymn for such an occasion', would not even be in the Top Twenty today, but it was chosen as the last hymn for Sangster's memorial service in the Central Hall – and I have chosen it as the last hymn for my funeral.

Let saints on earth in concert sing
With those whose work is done;
For all the servants of our King
In earth and heaven are one.

One family, we dwell in him,
One Church, above, beneath;
Though now divided by the stream,
The narrow stream of death.

One army of the living God,
To his command we bow;
Part of his host has crossed the flood,
And part is crossing now.

E'en now to their eternal home
There pass some spirits blest,
While others to the margin come,
Waiting their call to rest.

Jesu, be thou our constant Guide;
Then, when the word is given,
Bid Jordan's narrow stream divide,
And bring us safe to heaven.

APPENDIX A

❧ Further reading

Funeral Services of the Christian Churches in England (Canterbury Press, Norwich, new edition 1994): services for use at cemeteries and crematoria.

Funerals: A Guide – Prayers, Readings, Hymns, compiled by James Bentley, Andrew Best and Jackie Hunt (Hodder and Stoughton, 1994): by far the largest section in the book is entitled 'Readings'; a fascinating range of writings from different times and cultures.

Funerals and How to Improve Them by Tony Walter (Hodder and Stoughton, 1990) a sociologist looks at funerals in our society, and suggests how everyone involved in organising them can help to make them more meaningful and compassionate.

Making the Most of a Funeral by Jenny Hockey (Cruse-Bereavement Care, 1992): particularly of interest to ministers of religion and bereavement counsellors. Based on a study of the views and experiences of recently bereaved people and their ministers in Sheffield.

All in the End is Harvest edited by Agnes Whittaker (Darton, Longman and Todd, 1984): a series of texts, reflections and readings for those who grieve.

APPENDIX B

❧ Checklist when planning one's own funeral

Information which your next-of-kin and executor will need to know. (An excellent form of instructions relating to your funeral and other matters, to be acted on upon your death, can be obtained from Age Concern – see Appendix C).

- Where do you want the funeral service to take place?

- Who is to lead the service, read, lead prayers, preach?

- Choice of Psalms, readings, prayers, hymns and other music.

- If cremation, direction about the ashes.

- Any thoughts about memorials.

- Are flowers to be sent? – or donations sent to a charity?

Your next of kin will need to know about any pre-paid funeral plan, and about any plans or wishes to leave your body for medical research or organs for transplants.

APPENDIX C

❦ Useful addresses

Groups which provide help for the bereaved
Age Concern, Astral House, 1268 London Road, London SW16 4ER (0181-679 8000).
The Compassionate Friends, 6 Denmark Street, Bristol BS1 5DR (01272 292778). A national self-help organisation of bereaved parents, grandparents and children.
Cruise-Bereavement Care, 126 Sheen Road, Richmond, Surrey TW9 1VR (0181-940 4818). Largest bereavement care organisation in the world. Training. Publications. Direct Bereavement Line.
The Miscarriage Association, P.O. Box 24, Ossett, West Yorkshire WF5 9XG (01924 830515). For parents of a baby which is born dead before the 24th week of pregnancy.
Stillbirth and Neonatal Death Society (SANDS), 28 Portland Place, London W1N 4DE (0171-436 5881).

Organisations which deal with funeral enquiries
Crematorium Society of Great Britain, Brecon House, 2nd Floor, 16 Albion Place, Maidstone, Kent ME14 5DZ (01622 688292). Offers free and advice and help on any aspect of cremation.
National Association of Funeral Directors, 618 Warwick Road, Solihull, West Midlands B91 1AA (0121-711 1343).
Federation of British Cremation Authorities, Manor Park Cemetery, Sebert Road, Forest Gate, London E7 ONP (0181-534 1486).